Burt

"When Burt is attracted to a woman, his 'macho' demeanor changes. He drops his head a little, lowers his soft brown eyes, and smiles sweetly as he begins his flirtation. His target is immediately disarmed by his charm and the courtship begins."

Burt's Hair

"Burt's hair has always been a source of major discomfort and embarrassment to him. His hairpieces cost $1,500 and he needs a new one every week. He usually chooses to change them either by himself or in private with his hairdresser. Hopefully, one day he'll be happy with his own good looks. It certainly works for Sean Connery."

Burt's Women

"Part of the job was to prepare the house for visits by Burt's women. The houseman and I would check all the rooms, including Burt's bed linens, drawers in nightstands, dresser drawers, both bathrooms, even folded bath towels to remove any possible evidence that another woman had stayed over. Then, we were instructed to put out all the pictures and other mementos of the current girlfriend from carefully marked boxes."

BURT
and Me
My Days And Nights With
BURT REYNOLDS

Elaine Blake Hall

PINNACLE BOOKS
WINDSOR PUBLISHING CORP.

PINNACLE BOOKS are published by

Windsor Publishing Corp.
850 Third Avenue
New York, NY 10022

First Printing: November, 1994

Printed in the United States of America

Cover Photo: Courtesy of Lisa Smith, © 1994 by Lisa Smith

*To Mama and Daddy, Lori and Mickey,
Randy and Kim, Georganna,
and my five darling grandsons—
in order of appearance:
Stephen, Matt, Chris, Andrew, and Michael*

Acknowledgments

I would like to extend my deepest gratitude to Larry Kubik, who believed in me and gave me the courage to write this book, and to Ken Taylor, my knight-in-shining-armor, my "Kemo Sabay."

I'd also like to thank Carole and Jim Hampton; Mary and Budd Boetticher; Bobbie Ferguson; Ted Williams; Patty Morris; Michele Slate; Mark Bego; Tony Seidl; and Paul Dinas.

And a very special thanks to all my unnamed friends who supported me throughout this project.

And most of all to Burt Reynolds, who gave me an opportunity to share with him a life of "glitz and glamour" that most small-town girls only fantasize about and to travel an exciting, though sometimes scary, road to freedom.

TABLE OF CONTENTS

Introduction

For seventeen years I worked for Burt Reynolds as his personal assistant, secretary, social planner, and executive director of his year-round dinner theater. I was more like his mother than an employee. I selected and purchased his business and personal gifts, as well as hired and fired his house staff. I cooked for him, took care of him when he was sick, hostessed his dinner parties, and even covered for him when he chose to be unfaithful to his girlfriends and eventually his wife. As vice president of Burt Reynolds Productions, I was responsible for overseeing the development of his individual projects. I planned his wedding to Loni Anderson, scouted locations for his films, and was on call twenty-four hours a day—365 days of the year. When I am asked what qualified me to work for someone like Burt Reynolds, I always answer, "I raised three children . . . none of whom are in jail or dead!"

When in the 1990s, Burt returned to a weekly television series, Evening Shade, I moved to California to work with him on the show. By the second season of *Evening Shade*, I was promoted to the position of associate producer. When he starred in the 1992 movie *Cop and a Half*, I was the associate producer and referee between Burt and the director, the producers, and the crew members.

I have chosen to write this book to share with Burt's loving public, my experiences in his complex and diverse life as one of America's major celebrities. I hope this book will help people more clearly understand the warm, lovable, and delightfully humorous Burt Reynolds we all know and care about. In spite of the way he now portrays himself—as an arrogant, pretentious, hurt, and angry man—I know that underneath that facade, breathes a frightened and insecure individual who longs for public praise and superstar status.

As word started to circulate through the grapevine that I was penning the book you now hold in your hands, Burt had his current girlfriend, Pam Seals, call and make a very subtle inquiry. According to Pam, Burt said to her, "I hear Elaine's writing a book. Do you think she'll say anything bad about me?" Her reply to him was, "No, Burt, Elaine loves you and she would never say anything bad about you." Well, she's right. I do love Burt Reynolds, enough to write this book for him . . . and for me.

No, in this book there is nothing "bad" about Burt, but it is about the *real* Burt. If you don't recognize him, it's only because some of the stories I chose to include have never been told publicly before. The Burt Reynolds you'll meet here is the man whom his fans and admirers rarely see.

My life had been consumed by this celebrated and charismatic man, and I now invite you to join me as I relive those memories of Burt and me.

—Elaine Blake Hall

Private Secretary

I grew up in a fairly isolated area called Myrtle Grove Sound on the Intracoastal Waterway about twenty-five miles from Wilmington, North Carolina. The closest I had ever come to show business was sending away for a picture of Howard Keel when I was twelve.

I think one of the reasons Burt and I got along so well was because our backgrounds were somewhat similar. He grew up in Riviera Beach, Florida, in a small house. Although his father was the chief of police, his family didn't have a lot of money. His mother once told me that she actually made most of the schools clothes for Burt, his brother, Jim, and their sister, Nancy.

Despite our humble circumstances, I always planned to go to college and worked hard in school. However, that all changed when we got our first TV.

One night the most incredible show came on called *Private Secretary* starring Ann Sothern as

Susie. This woman was wonderful. She was bright, efficient, funny, took care of her boss, Mr. Sands, and solved everyone's problems in the office, in the office building, and out on the street. I knew right then and there I wanted a career as a "private secretary." I went back to school, canceled all of the required college-preparatory courses I was taking, and crammed in every business course I could get until graduation. I was hired immediately after graduation as secretary to the credit manager of Reed's Jewelers, a small chain of jewelry stores in Wilmington.

I got married and transferred with my husband, Herbert Millis, who was with the Seaboard Coastline Railroad, to Jacksonville, Florida. After he was killed in an automobile accident a few years later, I was left with two small children and I had to go back to work full time.

I landed a job as secretary to the vice president of a large paper manufacturing company for several years, married Jim Deacy, a very talented trumpet player, and moved to South Florida.

My association with Burt Reynolds began in February of 1973 at a square dance with our local Horseman's Association in Jupiter, Florida. Jim and I became friends with Burt's parents, "Big Burt" and Fern. Jim and Big Burt shared their love for the same music, stories, and bad jokes; Fern and I enjoyed discussing our children.

Fern would tell me stories about her son "Bud" as if he was still a teenager. Burt was called Bud by his family and in school was known as "Buddy." She and I had coffee at least twice a week at her house on Burt's ranch, and the four of us spent a lot of time together.

One day I was visiting with Fern, when "Bud" came out of the bedroom looking a bit drowsy and said, "Hi, you must be Elaine. Mama's told me so much about you."

I was surprised to see him and I casually responded, "Hi, Bud. I didn't know you were home."

He walked through the living room and into the study. Interestingly enough, as he passed me, I didn't see him as Burt Reynolds, the movie star, but I saw Bud my good friend's grown son. He was barefoot, dressed in a pair of jeans, and was not wearing a shirt, showing his very hairy chest. Strangely enough, before meeting Burt and having spent so much time with his mother discussing our boys, I guess most of the mystique of his being a "star" was gone.

A couple of years later when I was working for Burt, we discussed our first meeting. "Remember the first time I met you," he said. "You stayed about five minutes and got up and left. I thought you must have read something about me you didn't like or for some reason thought I was a real jerk."

I explained to him, "Heck no. I left because I felt it was the only time you had at home with your folks and you didn't need to share your time with a neighbor."

In the meantime, I had become friends with his older sister, Nancy, and we had been spending a lot of time together as well. One day Nancy informed me that Burt was receiving a lot of mail at his ranch and asked if I would be interested in working part-time as his secretary. I said yes and so began my time with Burt.

There's an old childhood saying I grew up with and still use. When I'm walking with anyone and we approach a person, tree, pole or whatever and it cuts between us, I always say, "bread and butter." I guess it's an old superstition, but supposedly the object or person would cut into a friendship, relationship, or whatever, unless you brought it back together with something that goes together. I noticed that Burt always said it too, when we were together, so I guess it worked for a long time.

In retrospect, I wonder how I could have expected others in my life to understand how working for Burt Reynolds could have ever taken priority over my family, my friends, and my own personal life.

It's really hard to describe the special relationship I had with Burt. I cared for him . . . almost as one does an unruly child. I excused his behavior at times, not because he was Burt Reynolds the celebrity, but because I knew and understood that the "child" in him was so very insecure and unhappy.

As time went on I came to realize that I had

fulfilled my dream and had become "Susie" the "Private Secretary"; unfortunately as I assumed her role, somewhere down the road I lost "Elaine."

Dinah Shore

Through my working with Burt, one of the first celebrities I met was Dinah Shore who was visiting the ranch at the time. I remember the first time I saw her I really was surprised at how tiny she was. She appeared much more statuesque on television. She was attractive, very friendly, and down-to-earth. She asked me about my family and whether or not we liked living in the country, and she gave me the feeling that she was genuinely interested.

I can truly say that among the women in Burt's life there was none "finah than Dinah." Burt, to this day, gives her credit for bringing him up from "Mullet" Reynolds of Riviera Beach, Florida, to a connoisseur of gourmet foods, fine wines, and so-phisticated music.

When Dinah came to Jupiter with Burt they stayed in his "tree house" on the back part of his 160-acre ranch. She decorated the tree house, as it is called today, a small intimate octagon-shaped building on a pedestal high above the ground with a spiral staircase just inside the entryway leading

up to the main floor. It has a raised wooden walkway up to the house with a gazebo about halfway
up. The entire house is glass all around affording
the occupants a breathtaking view of trees, birds,
and visiting wildlife. Dinah loved to cook and even
though the kitchen is quite small, it is well-
appointed with cooking gadgets and gizmos and
even a copy of her cookbook. The living room has
a complete sound system where they shared their
love for jazz. The only bedroom has glass windows
floor to ceiling with a king-sized bed overlooking
the beautiful Florida foliage and a pair of swans
leisurely swimming in the lake below.

Burt and Dinah loved to take long walks around
the property and rode horseback along the trails
in the sparsely populated wooded area surrounding the ranch.

Every time I saw them together, which was not
as often in the early seventies because they came
to the ranch to hide out and rest up from their
hectic schedules of television and films, they were
always smiling at each other and holding hands.
There was just something special about the way
they looked at each other. Dinah simply adored
Burt and doted on him constantly. I often wondered later on if perhaps she was too adoring and
he felt somewhat smothered and maybe that contributed to their breakup.

Burt appeared on the *Today* show in New York
with Barbara Walters in the seventies. As I watched
the interview, he was obviously uncomfortable and
slightly—although he'd never admit it—intimidated

by Ms. Walters. She made a comment about his romance with Dinah and the fact that although she was much older than he, the two of them seemed so happy together. She went one step further and asked why he didn't marry her.

Burt bristled and said to Barbara, "Why did you get a divorce?!"

"Wait a minute," she said, "I was told before this interview that I could ask you anything."

"You can, but not about that!" he replied. Burt was obviously incensed but realized that he was up against a pro, so he finally settled down and made some lame excuse that he wasn't ready for marriage. In fact he was already interested in someone else.

His then publicist David Gershenson made sure that he made up with Barbara Walters, because she was a powerful voice even in the early seventies. It paid off because several years later, she came to Florida and did a great interview with him in his home at Valhalla, Burt's estate in Hobe Sound, Florida, and gave a boost to his dinner theatre and the training program for young actors he had instituted. David deserves credit for keeping Burt out of trouble with the press for many years.

When Burt had his "Grand Opening" at the tack store and gift shop on his ranch in 1975, I was working behind the counter in the gift shop. Dinah and a few of his celebrity friends came to help celebrate with him and Dinah created quite a stir. I remember she was wearing blue jeans, a white blouse, and a red pullover sweater and stood out in a crowd of over ten thousand. People loved her and she always responded with a big smile. She and Burt signed autographs all day long.

Burt soon had to escape from the crowd and came behind the counter where I was standing. Women were pushing and shoving, almost crushing their own children to reach over the counter with T-shirts and pictures they had just bought in the store, scraps of paper, and anything Burt could autograph for them.

"Boy, they really love you!" I said.

"Well, it's a good thing," he said. "I don't know how to do anything else."

When Burt and Dinah broke up he just stopped calling her, changed all of his phone numbers, and was unable to face her for years. She was devastated according to Burt's mother and told her that she would "always love him." She was very close to Burt's mom and dad and stayed in touch with them even though she didn't talk with Burt. Burt had always said wonderful things about Dinah and they seemed so happy together that it was hard for his friends and the public to accept the breakup. Sadly, I don't think Dinah ever got over Burt.

In 1980, Burt invited Dinah to tape her television show at his theatre. As Burt's private secretary, I had an office at the theatre at that time. Before that, I worked for him out of an office in my home located a mile from his ranch.

During the show, Dinah and Burt were all smiles as they renewed their friendship.

Because Dinah was such a nurturer and had a

way of calming him down, they had many pleasant times together even though he was undergoing a lot of stress juggling his relationships with Sally and her, while cohosting Dinah's show, and performing every night at the theatre. We were doing *Same Time Next Year* at the theatre starring Burt and Carol Burnett and directed by Dom DeLuise. Dom and Carol both made stage appearances for the show and it was a hit.

Burt loves to sing and Dinah always encouraged him. She sang duets with him like "You Don't Send Me Flowers" and others she taught him. He once made an album called *Ask Me What I Am* in the seventies, and she assisted him, yet not revealing who she was on the album, listing herself only as a "friend." One day we received about five thousand eight-track tapes of this album to sell in the gift shop at the theatre. I really don't know how successful the sale of the album was in the music stores, but I do know there are a lot of eight-track tapes still stashed in a storage room in Jupiter, Florida.

In 1989 when Dinah was visiting friends in Palm Beach, she called me at the theatre and asked to reserve Burt's private box for her, a couple of friends, and Burt's sister, Nancy. At that time she was not aware that Burt's sister still wasn't speaking to me due to a misunderstanding ten years before. She and I talked for quite a while and she even invited me to join her group that evening. I quickly made the excuse that I couldn't because I had made a previous engagement. She asked that I at least stop by and say hello, so I told her that I'd try.

I called Burt and asked him what I should do. I was crazy about Dinah, but I knew his sister would probably get angry if I was there. Burt told me to call Dinah and just explain the situation so she wouldn't feel I was avoiding her. "Dinah knows Nancy very well and she'll understand, trust me."

Burt was right, Dinah was very sympathetic and said, "Honey, Nancy is a very unhappy woman, and there is nothing you can do to make it better. I'm sorry I won't get to see you, but I'm glad you called and explained."

The next time I saw Dinah was when Burt made an appearance on her talk show in 1990. When they first reunited, she told him, "When I pulled into my parking space on the lot and saw our names side by side again, it really got to me."

"It did to me, too," Burt said.

During the show they reminisced about some of the great times together and then he told her, "If I ever had one ounce of class, I got it from you."

"No, honey," she said quietly, "you've always had it."

After the show, I sat in the "green room" (the private room where celebrities relax while waiting to go on a show), and they talked, laughed and reaffirmed how much they cared for each other. They were sitting side by side on a small sofa and watching them squeeze each other's hand as they said the words, it was pretty obvious to me that they had never stopped loving one another. As he started to leave her, they hugged each other and held on for a long time as if each one hated to let go first. There was no impassioned kiss, but a very short, yet sweet one as they parted.

When Dinah passed away in 1994 I called Burt. His girlfriend Pam Seals answered the phone. They were living together in a house Burt had rented in Encino.

"He's so upset," she said. "He's closed himself up in his bedroom and won't come out or talk to anybody. I wish there was something I could do, but he knows I'm here for him. He really must have loved her a lot!"

Yes, Pam, he really did, probably more than he ever has any woman.

Tammy Wynette

Burt and Tammy had their first date in 1975 when he appeared on a talk show in Nashville with his longtime friend Jerry Reed. He was still dating Dinah at that time, but had an eye for Tammy and according to her, she fell for him hook, line and sinker.

I always wondered how these high-profile celebrity men could expect to get away with juggling high-profile celebrity women or vice versa. Until Pam Seals, Burt usually was involved with whoever his leading lady was or someone like tennis star Chris Evert or a former Miss America. Oh, he had many short-lived romances with a few women outside of the public eye—if they had big calves—but mostly he was attracted to women celebrities. He always told me that women with big calves drove him crazy! I guess that's why he and I were never attracted to each other. I like men with long legs—his are short and I was born without large calves.

Burt had been dating Tammy for a while and his parents were crazy about her. She came to the

first anniversary celebration of the opening of the
BR Ranch Tack and Feed Store in 1976. Burt,
Tammy, and his parents were seated upon an old
horse-drawn hay wagon that day and watched the
local cowboys and cowgirls compete in a horse race
around his racetrack. Tammy and Burt gave out
the trophies to the winners and smiled and had
their pictures taken all day long. I think just about
everybody in the county came to watch the special
event. I remember standing by the wagon and
looking around at the crowd. No one was watching
the race, they were all watching Burt and Tammy,
but then that's really why they all came in the first
place.

Tammy was really good for Burt. She was a typi-
cal Southern belle, brought up to "Stand by her
man." She was nurturing and loving throughout
the relationship. However, Tammy was so involved
with her kids and family, it was a bit taxing on her
romance with Burt.

Tammy wanted to be close to Burt when he came
to Jupiter, so she bought a house in Jupiter Inlet
Colony right on the ocean. The house was big
enough for her mom, all her kids, their husbands
and boyfriends to come and stay. However when
Burt was in town, she would choose to spend her
time with him exclusively. She kept her house in
Nashville as well and stayed there most of the time
when she wasn't on the road touring.

In the early seventies, Burt had made arrangements to celebrate his mother and father's fiftieth
wedding anniversary with a special party at the

Holiday Inn (now the Jupiter Hilton) on Jupiter Beach in the banquet room on the ninth floor overlooking the ocean. It was an exciting evening and all of Burt's family members and his parents' close friends were invited.

On the night of the gala event, everyone showed up . . . except Burt. It seems he got sick and had to stay in Los Angeles. I was really surprised he wasn't there, because I knew he was feeling fine the day before and even his folks were expecting him. At that time I wasn't aware his romance with Tammy had begun to wane. I learned from his family that this was a pattern for Burt when he couldn't face an uncomfortable situation.

Tammy was visibly upset the night of the party as were a few others because Burt didn't show, but his parents seemed to shrug it off with a "Well, that's Bud for you." They always accepted whatever he did or said.

Tammy wrote an especially beautiful anniversary song for them and when she sang it at the party, it really brought on the tears, including her own. But Tammy is a trouper and after she finished her song, she graciously hugged Burt's mom and dad and tried to mix and mingle for a few minutes, then quickly excused herself. The woman who had formerly worked for the hotel and helped organize the party said Tammy went into another room and sobbed, "Why didn't he come? Where is he?" and tried to call him in California, but was unable to reach him.

Actually, at that time, he was already involved

with Sally Field. He had Dinah Shore, Lucie Arnaz, Lorna Luft, and Chris Evert all worked in somewhere, but I can't honestly remember how they were juggled. You'd never know he missed the anniversary party though, because he had the family photo that had been taken at the party sent to Los Angeles so his photo could be added into the picture. It still hangs in the living room of his parents' home at the BR Ranch in Jupiter. He's standing right there with his sister, his mom and dad, his brother Jim and Jim's former wife, looking just like he was there all the time!

Losing Burt really broke Tammy's heart and even today, when she performs in Burt's hometown area and sings "Till I Can Make It On My Own," she always explains that it is a song she wrote when she and Burt broke up. "Ritchey" as Tammy affectionately calls her husband and manager, George Ritchey, was her musical composer and piano player when she was dating Burt. He doesn't mind when she announces the song that way to the audience because he feels it makes it more meaningful.

After all these years, Tammy has remained a true friend to Burt. When we needed money for the Burt Reynolds Institute for Theatre Training, we could always count on Tammy to do a benefit performance. If she had concert gigs scheduled within the South Florida area, Ritchey always called to let us know, so we could plan on a benefit concert for the Institute. Tammy is one of the finest ladies in our industry, always giving, and never taking.

When we were starting out on the "bus and truck tour" of Burt's one-man show in 1991, Tammy was on hiatus from her own tour and she allowed us to use her two buses to begin our tour. One bus was brand-new and Ritchey even sent his driver along.

When we did our show in Nashville, we spent the night in their home. It's a beautiful two-story mansion and is very warm and "homey." We sat up until late just talking and laughing and then I went upstairs to my room for the night, settling into a warm cozy bed.

Tammy's mother was in a hospital bed in a bedroom downstairs. She was near death and appeared to be comatose; however, Tammy insisted she spend her last days with them at home. She had a nurse twenty-four hours a day, but Tammy, Ritchey, and her children continually visited with "Meemaw" and talked to her even though it appeared she couldn't hear anyone. When Tammy walked into the room and began speaking, her mother gave a weak, faint smile.

During our time there, Burt and I went in to visit her. Tammy held her hand and spoke softly and lovingly to her, telling her that Burt was in the room with her. She managed another smile and he was visibly moved. Tammy told me later, "Meemaw always loved Bud, I'm so glad he came in to see her." She died shortly after our visit. Burt told me later that it was really hard for him to go in and see her, because he knew that his own mother, who was approaching ninety, would soon be passing on.

Although I no longer work for Burt, both Tammy and her husband have remained friends with Burt and me. This type of loyalty is rare in show business, but not for someone as sincere as Tammy.

The Burt Reynolds Horse Ranch

In the mid-sixties, Burt bought 160 acres about ten miles west of Jupiter, Florida. He loved the land and one of his dreams was to have a ranch, so he fixed up the old frame house, allegedly once a hideout for the Al Capone gang when the heat was on during Prohibition. His mother and father moved into the house and Burt went into the cattle business. He hired a ranch hand to take care of the black Angus he had bought, but the cattle did not prove to be lucrative, so he soon sold them.

He had always loved horses and listened when a friend once mentioned that Appaloosas (horses that have small spots on their rear or Leopard Appaloosas that are white with black or brown spots all over their bodies) were a special breed and when mated with thoroughbred horses were great for racing. Burt decided to breed them hoping to get a higher price when he sold the offspring because of his own celebrity.

Unfortunately, if the foal was born without any spots, it could not be registered as an Appaloosa, and since one of the parent horses was an Appaloosa, the horse could not be registered as a thoroughbred. Burt had quite a few horses born on his ranch that he could neither race nor sell at top dollar, because they were born without spots. These horses just became another financial burden to the ranch and were given to charitable organizations for auctions or sold for less than the costs of their breeding and care. After the death of his prize Leopard Appaloosa stud, Navajo Breeze (valued at over $100,000), Burt lost interest in the breed.

He had also become enamored with Arabian horses after meeting with Wayne Newton, who raises Arabians. He named his first mare Cat Dancing after the movie he made in 1973. Actually he named most of his horses after film titles and celebrity friends. He raised Arabian horses for a while, but soon the expense involved in feeding, veterinarian bills, and general care outweighed any profit-making dreams Burt had and he was forced to get rid of almost all of the horses left on the ranch.

Dinah Shore had a beautiful Appaloosa named Miss September and she won quite a few races all over the state of Florida. Burt wanted to have winning horses also, so he had a training arena and track built at his ranch. It was really an exciting time for all the neighbors who lived near the ranch, and many of us would go to the track to see the horses from the ranch that we had watched grow up now running at Pompano Racetrack. Unfortunately, his dreams of having a champion racehorse never materialized and the expense of training and racing killed that joy for him.

In 1975 when Burt held the grand opening of his feed and tack store, the exit off the Florida Turnpike had to be closed because the traffic to the ranch was so heavy. The tack store also was filled with Burt's movie memorabilia and souvenir T-shirts, ashtrays, jewelry, and hundreds of other items for fans.

In the late eighties when Burt was producing the game show "Win, Lose, or Draw" with actor Bert Convy, he decided to film it at his ranch in Jupiter. The ranch became a beautiful background for the show. Many stars came in to play the game that week and Burt was in his glory. Showing off the ranch to his Hollywood friends was something he reveled in. Burt made sure that his prize Arabian stallion, Cartouche, was prancing around in the background while the show was being filmed and that the lake, barns, and his folks were on film so he could share it all with the television audience.

Today the ranch provides a tour beginning with a movie in Burt's private screening room, then buses drive over the ranch property and the fans are shown actual locations where *Smokey and the Bandit II, The Man from Left Field,* Disney's *Flight of the Navigator,* and several episodes of ABC's *B.L. Stryker* series, were filmed. Next, Sound Stage II where many commercials and music videos are filmed, such as the Allman Brothers' hit album, *Where It All Begins;* the chapel where Loni and Burt were married; Burt's private office and much more. Thousands of tourists visit the BR Ranch each year and he is very proud of it.

All the World's a Stage

Burt has always loved the theatre. He began his career in theatre at Palm Beach Junior College in West Palm Beach, Florida, under his mentor, the late Dr. Watson B. Duncan and from there he moved to New York City.

Television and movies have occupied most of his professional life; however, he began to come back to Florida and direct plays in a little theatre in Port Salerno, just north of Jupiter. I met Sally Field for the first time at that theatre. Burt was directing *Bus Stop* and she, Robert Urich, James Best, and Maggie Mahoney (Sally's mom) made up the cast. The theatre was located adjacent to a railroad track and every night during the performance they had to stop until the train passed. Each night one of the cast members took the liberty of ad-libbing something about the train. The actors all enjoyed doing live performances and Burt loved directing them, so he decided to build a theatre of his own in Jupiter.

During the seventies, Burt was the number one

box-office star in America. *Smokey and the Bandit* was out and a big hit all over the country; *Hooper, The End,* and *Semi-Tough* were already out and making big bucks; and *Starting Over* was in the can ready for the theatres that year. Burt Reynolds was flying high in his career and now, the icing on the cake . . . his own theatre!

He wanted a place where blue-collar folks could afford to experience live theatre. Recognizing that most of his patrons would barely have enough time to get home from work, find something to eat and still make it to the show before the curtain went up, Burt decided to open a dinner theatre. He never liked the idea because he did not want actors competing with coffee cups and clinking glasses and because experienced performers often refused to work at dinner theatres. But, since Jupiter was a small town with few restaurants at the time, he realized that a dinner theatre was more practical.

On January 20, 1979, the Burt Reynolds Dinner Theatre opened with a black tie gala party. Newspapers and magazines from across the country came to celebrate. It was an exciting night that Burt shared with his many celebrity friends. Everyone was moved when he dedicated the theatre to his mother, Fern.

However, the opening was not all glitz and glamour. Like most dinner theatres, we served a buffet. The woman Burt hired to be General Manager was from the Deep South and arranged for a "down home" menu of fried chicken, stewed tomatoes, okra and cornbread. If you've ever tried to eat fried chicken wearing long white evening gloves like some of those Palm Beach socialities, it can be a real mess. Needless to say, the General Manager was fired a couple months later because of her continued poor management.

I was Burt's "East coast" secretary. I handled his personal correspondence and the fan mail that came to the ranch and worked out of my home about a mile from the ranch. When Burt came to Jupiter, he stayed at the ranch in "Bud's pad" as his folks called it. It was a little bungalow attached to the back of his parents' house with a screened breezeway between the two.

After the woman who had been managing the theatre was fired and the assistant manager moved into that position (he also only lasted a few months), I continued to work out of my home and also utilized Burt's private viewing box at the theatre as an office. But he began receiving a lot of mail at the theatre that required my working there as well. Soon I moved to a desk in the bookkeeping department upstairs at the theatre where his sister, Nancy Brown, was head bookkeeper.

Nancy left the theatre after a disagreement with Burt in the fall of 1979, and I became Burt's eyes and ears at the theatre. Over the next year he gained confidence in my business acumen. Then one day he called from California out of the blue and said, "You've really done a helluva job for me down there. You're not just a secretary, but I still want you to continue to do that for me. However, you've been running things there and I want you to have the title of Executive Director."

"Gee, thanks, Boss, but I think you need to get somebody who has more theatre experience than me. I can just continue to do what I've been doing and still be your secretary—that's enough for me. I love this job and I don't need the badge," I responded.

"Dammit! Nobody said you *had* to have the title, I just felt like you earned it and when you make a decision you don't have to say to everybody, 'Burt said to do this,' you will have the power to do it on your own!"

"I'm sorry, Boss. I didn't mean to seem ungrateful. Did I hurt your feelings?" I asked.

"Yes, it was like I gave you a present and you told me you didn't like the color," he said.

"I'm sorry, I just didn't think about it like that. I really appreciate the promotion and I'd be proud to be executive director of your theatre," I responded.

"Good! Damn, Elaine, it's hard to do anything for you!" he said.

When Burt redecorated the theatre in June of 1982, I moved into a new office upstairs with a beautiful desk and furnishings, sitting over the largest trap door in the building!

When we did *Death of a Salesman* with Julie Harris and the late Vincent Gardenia, directed by Charles Nelson Reilly, Burt insisted that we remove all items from the tables just before showtime. This created a bit of anger with some die-hard patrons who didn't want to comply. Many nights in the beginning, a few patrons actually threw their drinks in the face of their waiter. On those occasions, with our security person to back me up, I returned the patron's ticket price and suggested they stop on the way home and pick up a six-pack and some potato chips, go sit on their couch, watch television and belch.

During the summer of 1982 we created a separate dining room for the patrons who purchased "preferred seating" tickets and they filled the over one hundred and sixty theatre seats in front of the stage. This created a genuine theatre atmosphere for the actors on stage and with the clearing of the tables behind those seats at curtain time, it encouraged more big-name actors to perform at Burt's theatre.

We established a special clause in our contract with Actor's Equity that enabled us to pay only $2500 per week to the top stars in our productions. There is no way on God's green earth that we could have gotten stars like Sally Field, Carol Burnett, Martin Sheen, and the many big-name celebrities for that kind of money had it not been for their friendship with Burt.

When the producer and I were preparing to select shows for the next season, I'd call Burt and give him our suggestions for plays and stars. He'd decide which ones to produce and sometimes make his own suggestions. If he didn't like a star we had selected he'd nix it and suggest two or three more. Sometimes he would just call up and say he had run into a friend at a party and he wanted to do a certain play starring that person. We switched around the schedule to accommodate the celebrities who agreed to perform.

I spoke with Burt at least once a day, sometimes two or three times when he was at his home in California or on location for a movie. When he was in Florida, of course, I saw him every day and we talked on the phone constantly. He stayed involved with the theatre on a day-to-day basis, casting, selecting or approving the productions for the season. After every opening night, I had to call him immediately after the show to give the "bathroom reviews." I started doing this on my own because Burt always got upset if the reviews in the newspapers were bad. The ladies' room is always the best way to find out if the show is going well. There is always a line waiting no matter how many stalls you have, so there is constant chatter about the show during intermission and afterwards.

One of the main reasons Burt wanted a theatre of his own was to establish a place for aspiring young actors to develop their craft. So, he developed The Burt Reynolds Institute for Theatre Training. In addition to having classes taught by many of Burt's celebrity friends, the apprentices—we called them our "kids"—assisted in running the shows, appeared in many of the theatre productions, as well as their own productions and graduated a year later. Burt loved the kids and really enjoyed teaching them whenever he was in town. The classes usually were held after the show came down around eleven at night and continued until four or five in the morning. I loved sitting in on his classes and I saw that he had tremendous patience with each student and that they adored him. I thought many times how great it would be if he had that same kind of patience with his directors and peers in his television shows and movies and afforded them the kind of respect he received from these kids. He would probably still be on top today.

Many times he'd call me from California or wherever and ask me to contact the director of the Institute and schedule class time in the rehearsal hall so he could teach when he came into town. The kids prepared scenes with two or three apprentices and put together their own props and wardrobe from the scene shop. As each group finished performing, Burt made suggestions as to how they could improve the scene. He would direct them to change their position and delivery of dialogue, explaining to the class as he did so what the change would bring about to make the whole scene more believable. Burt is a really great teacher and it was amazing to see the improvements in these young actors throughout the year.

As a whole, every class was pretty great, but some had special situations that brought them closer to us. The graduating class of 1990 was a special group. They were like a family. I had left the theatre by then and was working with Burt on *B.L. Stryker* during their year, but my position with Burt afforded me the pleasure of being the "Mother" figure. When they had problems, needed money or advice, or just a hug, they came to me and I loved all of them.

One young and very talented actor, Scot Heminger, had such a great personality that everybody was crazy about him. Burt had already singled him out as one of the most talented young actors we'd ever had in the program, and after seeing his performance in *The Elephant Man* on stage, he was sure of it. One night around 7:00 P.M., I received a call that Scot had been hit by a car while riding his motorcycle to the theatre and was in the emergency room at Jupiter Hospital. I rushed over and joined all of the apprentices in the waiting area for word on his condition. Burt and Loni were married at the time and they came over and stayed with us for quite a while. We said a special prayer for Scot, and Burt and Loni went home so I stayed with the kids until we received the news.

The doctor finally came out in the wee hours and asked me to come into another room to tell me Scot had passed away. I couldn't believe Scot was dead and it was so hard to tell the kids. We all cried and held each other and then I had to call Scot's mother in Missouri. It was the hardest thing I've ever done. When I found out that she was alone at the time, I kept talking to her on the phone until Scot's girlfriend, who was in the same class, could call someone to go over to her home to be with her. We must have talked close to an hour. We both cried as she talked about him as a little boy and shared wonderful stories with me. Every time she said, "I can't believe my baby's gone and I'll never see him again," it broke my heart. What do you say to a mother when that kind of tragedy occurs? There are no words.

I called Burt after I hung up and he cried. He and Loni came to the special memorial service we held for Scot in the chapel at Burt's ranch, and we all laughed and cried as we reminisced about this special guy who had become such a part of our family.

I have stayed in touch with as many graduates as possible from all the classes since 1979 and I still attend plays in Los Angeles in which some of "our kids" are appearing. Every now and again, I get a call from some of them just bringing me up to date on their career moves.

Company's Coming

Every time any of Burt's celebrity friends were in town, they usually came to the theatre and we had to "clean up the house." Back home in North Carolina where I grew up, it was an unspoken rule that when "company's coming" everybody in the house was involved in cleaning up. Everything was always pretty clean anyway and you just dusted a little and put out the doilies.

It was really exciting when Red Skelton came to the theatre in 1979 to see *The Rainmaker* starring Burt and Sally Field. I always felt when I saw him on television that he probably was a very gentle soul. After meeting him, I knew I was right. I loved his television shows and I loved his artwork. Burt had collected several pieces including the ones of Carol Burnett and Lucille Ball. He drew one of his famous clown faces on a white cloth dinner napkin for Burt and Sally. I wish I had one of those today, but because of my position, I would never have asked him to draw one for me. Actually, during my many years with Burt, I have very few pictures of me with celebrities. I always felt that I was there to make Burt's friends comfortable so they did not have to play "celebrity," and didn't bother to get an autograph or have my picture taken with many of them.

In February of 1980, Burt called me from his house in Jupiter. "Marty (Martin) Sheen is coming to do *Mister Roberts* and his kid, Emilio, is going to be in the show as well. Emilio has never done anything before, but Marty says he has great potential and wants him to get his feet wet on stage," Burt said to me.

"Well, that's what you built this place for, Boss," I responded.

Emilio appeared to be as comfortable on stage as his dad and really did a great job. It's quite interesting to see how his career has flourished and even more so that of his brother, Charlie Sheen, who was studying to be an accountant at the time he attended one of the performances.

Burt took one look at Charlie and told him that with his looks and obvious talent, he should definitely become an actor. Charlie told Burt that he was not interested in becoming an actor and intended to pursue a career in business . . . but as you know, he changed his mind.

"Blues, my favorite colors are the Bl-oo-zz," Eartha Kitt sang from her heart onstage in *Cowboy and the Legend* at Burt's theatre in September of 1980.

On first meeting her, one senses that this powerful legend's eyes bear the scars of many years of racial discrimination and humiliation, masked in a very cold, distrusting stare as she speaks.

"She's a tough lady," Burt had said on the phone from his house in California. "She doesn't trust anybody and you won't get close to her, so don't take it personally."

Burt was dead right. However, in Burt's absence, it was my job to play hostess, and with Eartha in residence, I really had my hands full. I was naive enough to think that James Torrie, the house manager, and I could at least make her comfortable.

One night after the show, a small group of us went to the Log Cabin, a barbeque place in Jupiter near the theatre. Eartha never went anywhere without her tiny black poodle and she carried him around in her cloth purse. When we arrived at the restaurant, she casually lifted him out and placed him on her lap. While the young waitress was taking our order, she glanced down at Eartha's lap and asked, "Is that a dog?"

"No!" Eartha answered coldly. "It's my wig!"

"Oh, I thought I saw it move," the waitress said.

"Well, it didn't!!" Eartha said in an icy steel voice. The waitress didn't ask any more questions. Eartha had a look that could stop a springing mountain lion in midair!

Although we never became particularly, "chummy," I did find her to be a fascinating character who has lived a rough life, and is admirable as a self-determined survivor both in show business and in life. On one occasion during the run of the play, I listened to her describe her childhood growing up in the cotton fields, how she managed to overcome monumental obstacles as she forged her way through life to finally claim her just dues of fame and fortune, and how she was continuing to struggle to hang on to every thread of decency and respect she had worked so hard to attain.

"When Kirstie (Alley) gets here, put her in 205 Bermuda and Parker (Stevenson) in 304 Bermuda. They're basically married to each other, but Parker is a 'neatnick' and Kirstie is more like a 'beatnick,' so they may need separate apartments." Burt was speaking of two of the cast members of *Answers*, the show we were producing at his theatre, and directing me to put them up in his condos in Jupiter Harbour.

The show opened in October 1982 so Kirstie and Parker decided to have a Halloween party. It was a blast. They had decorated Parker's condo and were in costume as Dracula and a wicked witch.

Mary Anne and Charlie Durning and his daughter, Ned Beatty and his wife and son, Dom DeLuise, Karen Poindexter (the producer at Burt's theatre), Greg Hauptner (hairdresser to all the stars at the theatre), "Magic Lee" a local magician hired to entertain, and I made up the guest list. Burt and Loni were supposed to be there, but Loni called well into the party to say that Burt had gotten sick and had to go to bed so they were not coming.

"Well, that's strange," Kirstie said, "he was fine a half hour before the party when I called his house and told me he was definitely coming. Oh, well," she sighed and she made a certain gesture with her middle finger.

Parker and Kirstie were really a cute couple and had so much fun together. Kirstie and I had some really good girl talks. She was really funny and gave me instructions on how to keep a man. Obviously she knows what she was talking about because that was 1982 and she and Parker are still together and happily married with the children.

"I'll Never Speak to You Again."

Burt called me from California in January of 1979. "I need you to find a house on the ocean for me to rent. Sally and I will be doing *Rainmaker* at the theatre and I want a great place for us to stay while we are there." I had an active Florida Real Estate license so I began the search.

I found a beautiful home on the ocean in a safely guarded area of Jupiter Island and they both loved it. It was a brand-new house built by a sugar mogul who planned to use it as a vacation home with his family. I talked him into leasing it to Burt for a year for $50,000. This house had four levels and the property was secluded, so it was perfect for Burt. He stayed there while he and Sally filmed *Smokey and the Bandit II* and when he was either starring in or directing a play at the theatre until he bought Valhalla in Hobe Sound.

Many times Burt would call me over to the house to work on his correspondence. One night I got a call to come over to the house, and when I arrived Sally was downstairs in the kitchen cooking dinner. I don't know what it was, but it sure smelled good!

She said, "He really needs to talk with you and he's upstairs waiting."

When I walked into his bedroom, he was propped up on his bed in jeans and a chambray shirt. I sat down on the edge of the bed and Burt said, "Honey, this is very painful for me and I really need your help. I know you work with Nancy at the theatre and the two of you are good friends, but tomorrow I'm firing her boyfriend. She's going to be furious and will probably quit. You're doing such a great job and I really need you to help hold things together, so please don't quit, too."

Burt had hired his sister Nancy as head bookkeeper after firing the first general manager. He felt that since she was family, she would look out for his financial interests and he was right in that respect.

"This is really between you and your sister," I responded, "it has nothing to do with her friendship with me. I would never compromise my principles and quit a job just because someone else did. I've had to work all of my life and I would never leave without a valid reason. I'm sure she'll understand," I responded.

"No, she won't," he said, "you don't know her. I have to do it because he's not doing his job, but she'll probably never even speak to me again." I didn't believe him.

The next morning at work, Nancy went into a

meeting with the manager of the theatre and the producer. Burt did not attend the meeting, because he could never face a confrontation with anyone— especially his sister. Nancy was only gone a short time. When the producer tried to explain to her about the firing, she raced out of the meeting and came directly into my office. "Get your purse, we're leaving!" she said furiously.

"I can't leave now, I'm in the middle of something," I pleaded.

"I'll never speak to my brother again and I got you this job and if you don't get your purse and leave now, I'll never speak to you again as long as I live!" She stormed out of the office.

As I sat there, the phone rang. It was Burt. "Are you all right, honey?"

"No," I said. "I can't believe she did this. Surely she'll get over it and we'll still be friends."

"You don't know my sister, she'll hold a grudge for life."

Then Sally's voice came over the wire, "Don't you let them get to you, you are right and they know it. I'm proud of you for not giving in."

Well, I was glad I didn't "give in," but Burt was right. I've watched him do everything possible to gain his sister's love for almost twenty years, including giving her cars, houses in Florida and North Carolina, trips abroad, jewelry, and lavish gifts. Their relationship still runs hot and cold, and I hope, for his sake, that one day he'll succeed in winning her love.

As for her friendship with me? Nancy came back

to the theatre only once or twice since she stormed out in 1979. On these occasions Burt would have someone ask that I not be there, because it would upset her and to tell me he knew I'd understand. Whatever special event was taking place, even if I had arranged and planned it, if "sister" decided to go at the last minute, I was asked not to show up, because she "might walk out."

I had to take a "day off" if sister decided to visit the set of *B.L. Stryker.* When she visited the set of *Evening Shade,* while I was associate producer, I was asked to please stay in the office and not come on the set. And when I produced Burt's road show and she came to a performance in North Carolina, I was asked to "take the night off." Why did I allow it? She's his sister, I was an employee, that's why I always called him "Boss."

Sally Field

I first met Sally in the mid-seventies when Burt directed *Bus Stop* at the Manatee Theatre, a little theatre in Pt. Salerno, Florida. I went to the theatre with Burt's mom and his sister, Nancy, and I was really impressed not just with Sally's performance, but the way she made Fern, Burt's mom, who was quite shy, feel so comfortable. Fern commented on the way home that Sally was so cute and funny and that she liked her a lot.

When the Burt Reynolds's Dinner Theatre opened in January of 1979, Sally Field, Tyne Daly, and Gail Strickland starred in *Vanities*. I must say the language was a bit shocking to the "folks back home," but the cast and performances were so outstanding it was a sellout. Immediately following *Vanities*, Burt and Sally costarred in *The Rainmaker* at the theatre.

Sally had already filmed three movies with Burt: *Smokey and the Bandit*, *The End*, and *Hooper*, plus *Smokey and the Bandit II* was in preproduction. I always felt it may have put a strain on Burt and

Sally's relationship to be living and working to-
gether, and it showed. Burt's dad once told me,
"Bud always falls in love with his leading lady!"
Obviously he was right about Sally.

When Burt and Sally first started dating in 1976
during *Smokey and the Bandit* and were both in California, Burt's dad told me that once he got mad at
Sally. He called Burt's house in California and this
"young lady," as he put it, answered the phone. "I
want to speak to Bud," Burt, Sr., said to her.

"He's resting and not taking any calls right now,"
she replied.

"Well, this is his father and he always takes my
calls," he insisted.

She went away from the phone and came back.
"He'll have to call you back," she told him.

"Who is this?!" Burt, Sr., asked.

"This is Sally and he said to tell you he'll call
you back."

"Well, you go tell him I'm on the phone now
and I want to talk to him!" he said.

Burt's dad told me he felt Sally was putting him
off. I explained to him that it wasn't her fault, she
was just doing what "Bud" told her to do!

I loved it when Sally was in town and we went
shopping together. I always enjoyed going places
with her. She usually wore jeans, a T-shirt, and a
baseball cap. Everyone still recognized her and she
was great with her fans. On occasion someone who
was not quite sure it was really Sally would say to

her, "Does anyone ever tell you that you look just like Sally Fields?" (Usually adding an "s" to her name.)

"Yes, my mother does," she'd say with a smile, "because that's who I am."

She loved her two boys, Peter and Eli, and every time she came to Florida, one of the first things she wanted to do was shop for something special for them. Burt and Sally really loved each other and I think they would have gotten married, but he was afraid of taking on the boys.

Sally and her boys had a very close relationship and Burt was deathly afraid of it. Burt once told me that he was always afraid that if he and Sally got married and he tried to correct the boys that they would look at him and say, "You're not my father!" He said that he wouldn't know how to respond.

"It's simple," I told him, "just say, 'I know that, your mother knows that, and you know that, but what you're doing requires a father figure to correct it . . . and that's what I'm doing!' "

Burt really never wanted to face that kind of challenge, so the marriage never happened.

Sally and Burt were always getting mad at each other and breaking up. She was very open about her feelings and Burt couldn't intimidate her. She'd get angry at him, make plane reservations, call a car to pick her up, and say, "I'm outta here!"

Once in 1985 when she and Burt had gotten back together, we were just talking about kids and life in general and she asked me, "Didn't you say when you first married Jim Deacy, you had two small children and he had never had any children before?" I knew she and Burt had talked about getting married in the past, and I sensed they had been discussing the possibility again.

"That's right," I replied.

"How did you handle it?" she asked.

"It was an adjustment for all of us," I told her. "I was so close to the kids and they were very open about everything. Randy and Lori were seven and nine at the time and came to me one day and said that Jim was being unfair. I told them that since this seemed to be happening a lot, we would vote to see if he could stay. I said, 'Everybody in favor of getting rid of Dad, raise your hand!' I raised mine, and they looked a little dismayed. They decided that because he was funny, a good cook, and most of all, because they loved him, that we should keep him. We took another vote and kept him for another twelve years."

Sally said, "That's great, I love it."

"Are you thinking about marrying Burt?" I asked her.

"I don't know," she said softly. I didn't pursue the question and that night they had a fight and the very next day she went back to Los Angeles.

This particular breakup was probably the most significant. Loni was in the wings then, so Burt had someone to run to. Actually, Burt had already arranged for Loni to come to Jupiter as Sally left.

James Torrie, Burt's Scottish house manager, and I had a short time to take Sally's pictures down, remove all the little ceramic frog mementos (Burt called her "Frog" in *Smokey and the Bandit*) and get all of Loni's pictures up in the right spots and *her* little mementos out.

Burt always had James and me check everything. We kept boxes of pictures and mementos for each woman who had been in his life for a while. When he had a fight with one of them, James and I had to remove all pictures of her along with every little trinket or reminder. We awaited our cue from Burt as to whether we needed to put the same ones back out or get one of the other boxes and hang someone else's pictures, and place her little trinkets around. We always knew exactly where the pictures were previously hung, so they would be in the same place when his current lady friend came back. That was one of the "unspoken" prerequisites for the job, that you never forgot where everything went, because, believe me, the ladies remembered!

Sally did an interview with *Playboy* magazine later on that really upset Burt. It was not a bad article, but it didn't portray him as the kind of guy he wants the public to believe he is. He was so angry with her that he even made a few choice remarks on talk shows, and to my knowledge that marked the end of their relationship, and the two of them never had another reunion. Years later he finally came around and started talking about her in a more positive manner and admitted how much he had really cared for her.

After we had finished filming *Cop and a Half,* I was in my office at Valhalla with Burt. We were talking about how unhappy we both had been in our marriages for the past couple of years, and he said to me, "You know how much I loved Sally and I didn't marry her when I had the chance and I always regretted it. Don't you make the same mistake. If you really love somebody, do it then . . . don't wait and just settle for someone else."

"How do you feel about Pam Seals?" I asked.

"I love her to death. She is good to me and she's so honest. I just can't do anything about it now, I can't afford to divorce Loni," he said.

Miss Ida

Ida Turner was like a mama to all of us. She had worked all her life and put her own five children through college. She is a wonderfully spiritual African-American woman, who was the full-time housekeeper at Valhalla, and once a week she cleaned and fluffed everything at Burt's two beach houses in Jupiter as well.

"Miss Ida," as we affectionately call her, used to fix special "home remedies" for Burt when he was sick. He'd call me and say, "Please talk to her. I don't want to hurt her feelings, but I can't drink that stuff, it tastes awful!"

"I know, but it always works, so what do you care? Just hold your nose and drink it and get well," I'd say.

"Very funny," he'd respond. "I love her to death, but I'm just not going to take that stuff anymore, so please talk to her."

"Okay, Boss, you've got it."

When I told her he didn't want to take any more of her "home remedies," she said, "Honey, that boy needs help and I can help him if he'll just let me." She just kept on "fixing and mixing" and trying to take care of him in spite of himself.

After an automobile accident a few years ago, she was unable to work at Valhalla because of all the stairs. She still asks me every time I speak with her, "How's my baby? Is he doing any better? I still pray for him."

Charles Nelson Reilly came to Jupiter quite often to direct a play at the theatre or to teach the apprentices. His home away from home was the big beach house and Miss Ida was always there to take care of him and his houseguests.

Miss Ida loves life and gives it a special meaning. Many times when I was having a particularly difficult time in my personal life or as part of "Burt's World" she'd put her arms around me so tightly I felt my ribs would break. She would give me a big squeeze, then shudder and say, "Thank you, Jesus!" and continue, "The Lord just blessed you, child, now you're gonna be all right!"

Over the years she constantly reminded me, "Honey, when you're scared or hurt, just look to the East and say the Twenty-third Psalm and you'll be fine."

She was right and I do that even today. As I'm driving down the freeway I just say, "Lord, I have no idea if I'm going north, south, east, or west, but I'll say the words if you'll just point them in the right direction."

Farrah Fawcett

"I need you to finish the job, because I just fired the decorator." Burt was calling me from California. "If you need help, I can send someone from here, but I'd really rather not."

It was the summer of 1980 and Burt had purchased a beautiful Spanish estate, called "Valhalla," located in Hobe Sound on the intracoastal waterway just a few miles north of Jupiter, Florida. The house had been vacant for about ten months after the owner had died, so Burt contracted a local interior designer to refurbish it. She and Burt had a couple of disputes, so he released her and now I, the understudy, was going to play the lead. There was only one problem, I didn't have a copy of the script. However, Burt's comment about not wanting to send anyone from California was my cue to get it done.

I was at the house at 7:00 A.M. every day to supervise the resurfacing of the driveway, the interior and exterior painting of the house, two guest houses, duplex servants quarters, and the convert-

ing of a four-car garage into a rehearsal hall with
the "properly cushioned hardwood floors for danc-
ers." My deadline to complete this project was two
and a half weeks, because Farrah Fawcett, who had
recently filmed *The Cannonball Run* with Burt, was
coming to the theatre for her stage debut with
Dennis Christopher in *Butterflies Are Free*.

Burt had purchased the entire contents of an
old Georgian mansion to furnish the house, so I
arranged for someone to place the furnishings
when the vans arrived.

Everything was running at a frantic pace, but on
schedule. The day before Farrah was to arrive, my
then husband Jim and I spent the night in the
house to determine if there were any last-minute
details that had been overlooked.

Near disaster! fluorescent not incandescent lights
were over the makeup table in the "Hers" bath *and*
there was no outlet in which to plug in a hair dryer
and curling iron! I called the electrician at his home
at 6:00 A.M. the next day to come over and put in
an outlet. When the lighting fixture store opened,
I selected real makeup lights for both the "His" as
well as "Hers" baths.

All finished on time, we awaited Farrah's arrival.
When she got off the plane, she was smiling, wearing no makeup, had her hair pulled back in a po-
nytail, and looked absolutely beautiful. She was so
sweet to everyone, and we all really loved having
her around.

She's an excellent tennis player, so we arranged
to have the best players in the area play with her

on the court at Valhalla. When asked how her hair and face stayed so dry in the humid Florida weather after a particularly strenuous tennis match, she just flashed those big, white teeth and like a true Southern belle said sweetly, "Oh, I never perspire!"

All of the women within earshot took an immediate dislike to her . . . except me . . . because I never perspire either.

Burt was very appreciative that I was able to get the house done on time, and soon afterward a large box arrived at the theatre from Dicker and Dicker in Beverly Hills. Inside the box was a full-length Blackglama mink coat with a note that said, "Don't say a word. You deserve it! I love you, Burt."

I don't know what possessed me at that moment, but I quickly put the coat back in the box and into the trunk of my car. I kept thinking, *What in the world is he giving me this for? It's much too elaborate a gift for just fixing up a house.* I later learned that the decorator he fired had asked for her fee to be a small part money and the balance in a new Cadillac. I guess he figured since I was on salary that he'd give me the coat as sort of a bonus.

I immediately called Burt to thank him and he said, "You worked so hard to get that house done for me and I wanted to give you something I knew you'd never buy for yourself."

I left the fur in the box in the trunk of my car for a couple of months before hanging it in my closet. I dreamed one night that I was back home in our little house on Myrtle Grove Sound, where

I grew up, and I had my coat with me. All four of us kids slept in one small bedroom and there was no closet. We each had a large nail in the wall where we hung our clothes, and I dreamed that I had hung my fur coat on my nail one night. The next morning, all the fur was on the floor with the lining still hanging on the nail.

When I awakened, I decided that I'd better find a way to wear that fur coat in spite of my personal convictions and whether I thought I deserved it or not, because Burt Reynolds had spent a lot of money for it and he damn well expected me to put it on!

About six months later, Burt and some of his friends were in town and attended the graduation of the apprentices. It was one of the coldest nights in Jupiter and actually went down to forty-eight degrees. I put the fur coat in my car just before I left for the theatre in case I got enough nerve to put it on.

After the graduation exercises when most of the audience had gone home, I decided to go for it. Of course, I couldn't play it straight, so I put the coat on and engaged the dining-room manager to wheel me through the lobby on a cart from the kitchen, and I waved the "English Royal Wave" to those people in the lobby as I passed through, down the aisle of the theatre, and up on stage where Burt and his friends were gathered with the graduate apprentices just standing around chatting.

When he saw me, he burst out laughing and

came over to give me a big hug and said, "It looks great on you!"

"Thanks, Boss, it's very special," I said, but I never really wore it very much after that. It stayed in storage for years. Well, after all, I did live in South Florida, and it was the thought that really counted!

Elizabeth Taylor

"I need you to get a limousine to pick me and Elizabeth Taylor up in Ft. Lauderdale. She's coming down to see the theatre and maybe she'll do something down there," Burt's voice came over the phone. "We're flying into a private airport there and I'll let you know which one later. By the way, don't send Tony from Jupiter. He's a nice guy but that old Cadillac limo he's got may not make it back. Call somebody in Lauderdale and get a really nice one, okay?"

"Where will she be staying, at the house or a hotel?" I asked so I would know whether or not to do anything special.

"She can have my room because it's bigger and also has the ladies' bathroom. I'll just stay in one of the guest rooms," he said.

"You got it, Boss," I answered and hung up the phone. I called a limo company we used in Ft. Lauderdale and explained what I needed.

"Oh, it's for Burt?" the woman on the phone chirped. "I have just the one. It's very special and he'll love it. It's a white Mercedes stretch, so just tell me what I should stock drink and snack-wise and I'll take care of it."

I didn't see Burt until the next day when he came by the theatre. "How was the drive back from Lauderdale? Did you have a lot of traffic?" I asked, hoping he'd tell me everything went great and the driver was there on the tarmac to meet them.

"Where the hell did that car come from?" he asked.

Oh, crap! I thought. I had already checked with the woman at the limo company that morning and she said the driver told her they seemed to have a great time. "Why, wasn't it a white Mercedes?" I asked sweetly.

"It sure as heck was, a 1957 model that was about as subtle as the Rose Bowl Parade! When we started over to the car, Elizabeth looked at me and said, 'Where are the balloons?' The ride was similar to being on a covered wagon and we could feel every hole and rock in the freeway, but she was a great sport and we had a lot of laughs over it," he said.

It was the fall of 1980 and she had come for a short visit, attended Burt's theatre and visited with the apprentices. The evening at the theatre began with dinner in Burt's private box, which was a small dining room about 12′ x 15′. I always hired waiters for the private boxes upstairs who were not only skilled in fine cuisine and proper service, but would not discuss what went on in those boxes. I talked with the box waiter later that night to make

sure everything was going well and he told me that
"Miss Taylor was wearing a caftan and spilled her
drink in her lap and went into the bathroom (it
was located in the room) and removed her panty
hose and placed them in the trash can. I saw them
in there when I went in to change the towels and
freshen it up."

"Well, they'd better still be there tomorrow morning when I get in. I don't want to find out you've
framed them and have them on display at your
house!" I said.

After the show, Burt and Elizabeth joined the
apprentices in the rehearsal hall. We were doing
Babes in Arms with the class of 1980 and graduates
of the class of 1979. It was definitely not one of
our best productions, but she was very gracious to
the kids when she met them. It was obvious that
she and Burt enjoyed each other's company and
were having a good time together. I don't know
what happened between them to change that
status. I was not privy to that situation, nor aware
there was a problem between them until a short
time later.

When the producer of Burt's theatre, Karen
Poindexter, and I were heading for New York to
cast an upcoming show, we attended many plays—
on Broadway, off Broadway, and off-off Broadway
to stay current with what was going on in the theatre market. We were always allowed to visit backstage to meet the cast after the show. On one
particular trip to New York in August of 1981, I
told Burt that Elizabeth Taylor was appearing in

The Little Foxes and we were planning to attend. He said, "I haven't talked to her in a while. Please give her my love and my new phone number and ask her to call me."

When we were ushered into her dressing room, she was very sweet and said to me, "Just how is Burt these days?"

I smiled and handed her his private phone number saying innocently, "Oh, he's just great. He sends his love and would like you to call him."

She smiled sweetly and said, "Thank you so much for coming" . . . but I saw her hand curl around the paper and crumple it.

The next day, I told Burt that I had given her the number, and he said, "Was she mad? I haven't called her in a while."

"Oh, thanks a lot for sending me to the front lines!" I said. "I don't know whether she was mad or not, but she crumpled up your phone number!" He laughed a little sheepishly.

After a few weeks had passed, I asked Burt if Elizabeth had ever called him.

"Nope," he said, "but she sent me a plant, no note with it, just a plant." It was a very straight, tall cactus in the center, with a short round one on each side—I think he got the message.

Charles Nelson Reilly

One of Burt's very best friends is Charles Nelson Reilly. Like Dom DeLuise, Charles will drop whatever he is doing and come to Burt's aid whenever he needs something. Charles has been a devoted friend of Burt's for many years, and Burt could always count on him to direct a play, teach the kids at the Institute, throw a fantastic pasta party for four or a hundred, emcee a function or just tell a few jokes at a cocktail party. Charles makes Burt laugh. The two of them have a very special relationship.

Charles sat drinking a Manhattan at the kitchen table in Burt's house on the ocean in Jupiter, Florida, one day in 1980. I had picked him up earlier at the airport that day and we began a friendship that has lasted many years. He is not only a very talented actor and director, but an incredible teacher. His dedication to the Institute for so many years left its impact on young actors all over this country. I was privileged to sit in on many of his classes during my tenure at Burt's theatre. The results of his teachings were astonishing.

Charles only appeared in two productions at the theatre, *The Odd Couple* with Darryl Hickman and *Bye Bye Birdie* with Alice Ghostley, but directed eighteen productions, plus all the apprentice productions.

The first time Charles came to the theatre in late 1979, he took one look at the sleepy little town of Jupiter and said, "Does the bus even stop here?" As he began to spend more time at Burt's theatre and the Institute, he became a regular at the old truck stop/restaurant/gas station/Western Union/Greyhound Bus Stop . . . the hub of the community. He became so enamored with the theatre, that he still refers to Burt's theatre today as "A Miracle at a Truck Stop!" He even had bumper stickers made up, and we sold them in the gift shop at the theatre.

Burt could always count on Charles to come through for him in a pinch. We were doing *Answers,* written by Ernest Thompson, at the theatre, which consisted of three one-act plays and was a box-office hit for us. The first play directed by Charles Nelson Reilly starred Burt Reynolds and Stockard Channing; the second directed by Dom DeLuise starred Charles Durning and Ned Beatty; and the third directed by Crandall Diehl starred Kirstie Alley and Parker Stevenson.

Unfortunately, during the run of the play, Stockard became ill and was unable to perform.

"I can't do it with her stand-in," Burt said to me in the afternoon, "she just doesn't get it."

"Well, shall we get someone else in right now and you can go over the blocking and she can perform with the script in hand? The audience will understand," I offered.

"No," he said, "I don't think there is time to get the blocking done, and the only person who can pull it off would be Charles, if he'll do it."

"Is he doing it in drag?" I asked.

"I'll ask him if he will do it and he can decide what is more comfortable for him," Burt responded.

Charles elected to wear his own clothes so he chose a dark blue business suit and played it straight. We explained to the audience about Stockard's illness before the curtain went up, and they fell into the fun of it all. Charles was hysterical, and he and Burt played the characters exactly as written. The audience loved it and when the performance was over, they received a huge standing ovation.

As the curtain was raised for the entire company to take their bows, the audience again rose to their feet and applauded. As the group of stars held hands and took their bows together, they began to back away so the curtain could come down. Slowly the curtain began to descend, but then it slipped and fell down directly on their heads. The audience gasped, the stars burst into laughter, and the stage manager cried. It must have been an omen, because at a later date we tried to get the rights to produce Ernest Thompson's *On Golden Pond,* and he wouldn't permit it as he said we "ruined his play because Burt Reynolds had allowed Charles Nelson Reilly to play the female lead in *Answers.*

Carol Burnett

"Some of these people camped out all night in front of The Burt Reynolds Dinner Theatre to make sure they were able to get tickets for *Same Time Next Year* starring Burt Reynolds and Carol Burnett," the announcer said. The local television stations were showing film on the news of people with tents, beach and lawn chairs, picnic baskets, and drink coolers lined up outside the theatre. You can imagine the excitement it created in the little town of Jupiter at that time . . . Burt Reynolds, Carol Burnett, and the director, Dom DeLuise . . . megastars! We had not had this kind of response from the public since Burt and Sally Field did *Rainmaker* in 1979.

When I drove in to the theatre parking lot, I couldn't believe the line of people outside waiting to buy tickets. The first part of the line looked like a bunch of refugees who had just gotten off the boat at Ellis Island. It was January 1980 and even in South Florida it gets pretty cold during the night, so the early-morning crowd was wrapped in jackets and blankets. There were men who needed a shave, drinking coffee out of thermos bottles and plastic cups; women without makeup and their hair sticking out in all directions; one guy brushing his teeth, holding a plastic glass of water, and spitting in the parking lot, afraid to walk over to the grassy area for fear of losing his place in line; Then there were the "I know I'm going to be late for work, but I don't give a damn, I'll have tickets for this show" better-dressed group bringing up the rear of the line.

At Burt's theatre, we only had a two-week rehearsal period before a show opened and after the season subscribers had gotten their ticket orders in, it was "up for grabs" to the public.

In the ten years Burt had his theatre he only performed in three plays, one in 1979, one in 1980, and the last in 1982. He directed seven. It was due mostly to his fear of what the local critics would say about him. He kept an ongoing battle with the theatre critics of the two top newspapers, *The Palm Beach Post* and *The Miami Herald*. When he was out of town, he'd call and have me read him the reviews, and I would skirt around the bad parts and say, "Well, they weren't crazy about so and so," and read only the good lines as the critics wrote them.

Once he was asked in my presence how he felt about the local critics and he said, "Well, Elaine knows how I feel about those bastards, so she only reads me the good parts."

The South Florida Writer's Association is composed of theatre critics in all the publications in the southern area of Florida. Each year the "Carbonell Awards,"—their version of the Tony Awards—a beautiful bronze egg-shaped award with gold overlay and mounted on marble created by famous sculptor Manuel Carbonell, was presented by this group. In 1983 Burt directed Charlie Durning and Bill C. Davis, who was also the writer, in *Mass Appeal.* It was a fantastic production and that year it won several awards including Best Production, Best Performance in a Leading Role, Best Set Design, Best Lighting, Best Everything . . . except Best Director. That slap helped to solidify Burt's insecurity about the local critics, and it was four years before he directed another play at his theatre.

I arrived at the theatre the morning tickets went on sale and rehearsals were to commence for *Same Time Next Year.* I was feeling very excited myself about seeing Burt and Carol Burnett performing live on stage, and feeling very lucky not having to brush my teeth in the parking lot to get a ticket. The producer met me as soon as I arrived and said that Burt was in his box and was not feeling well and couldn't do the show with Carol, and she was on her way over to the theatre at that moment to see him. Dom DeLuise, the director, was trying to convince Burt that he should rest a little and then give it a shot. After seeing the line out front, I thought it was a little late to be "calling in sick."

I ran into Carol as she came up the stairs to meet with Burt. She had just gotten the news that Burt was not going to be her leading man and had a look of panic on her face as she passed me.

"Is he 'real' sick?" she asked.

"I don't know," I replied, sensing the real reason. "Maybe you can make him feel better."

Carol, with a little help from Dom, was able to convince Burt to do the show. The performance sold out immediately and was a smash hit. Carol was phenomenal as "Doris," and Burt was absolutely the best "George" I've seen. The two of them had a special spark that connected every time they were on stage and the audience loved them. Sure enough a critic from one of the major papers gave an overall good review, touted Carol's performance, but said that Burt was very "stiff" as George.

In 1988 Carol came back to Jupiter to see her daughter, Erin, who was appearing in *Nunsense*. Carol was having a major sinus problem at the time and asked me about seeing a doctor. She was flying out the next day and the pressure was always so great on takeoff and landing that she felt she needed something to clear her head.

I drove her to my ear, nose, and throat doctor during his off-duty hours, so she would not have to play "celebrity" when she wasn't feeling healthy. The doctor gave her the necessary medication and told her to suck a solution of warm saltwater up her nose and let it drain out and honk before taking the flight and then just before landing. She and I had quite a laugh as she demonstrated in the car how she would do this in front of the passengers on the airplane, pretending she was strapped in her seat in first class.

On the way back from the doctor's office, Carol and I talked about how difficult it was at our age to enter another relationship with a man, and most especially in her circumstance as a celebrity.

Carol Burnett is one good-looking gal with a fabulous personality, so why aren't men beating down her door? Well, they are, but as she said, it's so hard to find one you can really trust who is interested in her as a person and not as a star.

Carol told me that she had finally reached a point where she would call a male friend just to escort her to a party or function to keep from going alone. We both agreed that as much as we loved having someone special in our lives, that it was almost too scary to entrust our hearts.

I saw Carol again at a barbeque at Burt's house on Mullholland Drive in Los Angeles in 1991. Burt and Loni had invited some of the cast members from *Evening Shade* and a few friends over. No, Burt was not outside in a "Born to Bar-B-Que" apron slaving over a hot grill. In fact, no one was cooking. Clarence, the cook who was on staff at the house, bought the barbecued chicken and ribs at Tony Roma's and everything else from the deli in Gelsons market.

Burt greeted his guests in a sports jacket and cravat, Loni was in a beautiful silk outfit, and everyone else was dressed as advised in various stages of "California Casual" which is definitely upscale from "down-home casual."

I said to him when I arrived at the house in a silk blouse and slacks, "I feel pretty dressed up for a barbeque, but Loni said this was the attire for the evening."

"It's perfect," he said. "Nobody wears dungarees to anything anymore."

Dungarees? I thought. *Nobody* says *"dungarees" anymore either!*

Carol arrived in a very casual, but darling blue jeans outfit and took one look at everybody and said, "I thought this was a barbeque!"

Me, too, Carol, I wanted to say.

Patty Fuller

Patty Fuller, an incredible interior designer and longtime friend of Burt's, had decorated Burt's house on Carrolwood Drive in Holmby Hills outside of Los Angeles, and it appeared in *Architectural Digest* in 1973. He has depended on her expertise and talent to decorate several of his residences for many years. She once confided in me that they had a short-lived romance that was never consummated. They found that their friendship was more important to the both of them and the spark quickly died.

Once in 1983 Burt came home to Florida and walked out onto the veranda of his home at Valhalla. I followed him outside, because I could tell he was upset. "What's the matter, Boss?" I asked.

"Patty has hurt me so badly, and I don't understand it," he said.

"Patty Fuller?" I asked. She was the only Patty I knew that was close to Burt, and she and her former husband, Robert Fuller, who starred in *Wagon Train* and *Emergency,* had been close friends with him for over twenty years.

"Yes," he said quietly. "I gave her a beautiful fur jacket for Christmas and she sent it back to my house with the meanest letter I've ever gotten."

"You're kidding, that doesn't sound like Patty," I said, "I'll call her and find out what happened."

"When you call her, tell her I can't believe she would hurt me like this after all I've done for her and not to try and contact me, because it's too painful for me." Burt always turned these kinds of situations around so that he became the victim.

"Okay, Boss, I'll call her." I had to find out what happened between them. When I called Patty in California she told me that Nancy Streebeck, Burt's secretary on the West coast, had called her and said, "Burt wants me to pick up a fur jacket for you for Christmas from him. Do you want to go over to Dicker and Dicker and pick one up yourself? It'll save me a trip."

Patty replied, "Forget it, I don't want to go pick out my own gift from him. I don't want anything from him."

Patty said that just before Christmas, a box from Dicker and Dicker was delivered to her house and inside was a fur jacket and a typed note from Burt and signed in Nancy's handwriting. She promptly packed up the jacket and sent it back to his house with a note telling him how insensitive she thought he was. It was a known fact that when Burt was ending a love affair, that he gave the departing girlfriend an expensive gift, usually a car or a fur coat, so therefore she felt that was her farewell gift.

I had developed a personal friendship with Patty, so I continued to stay in touch with her, plus I knew Burt would get past what had happened between them. Patty was too honest and had meant too much to Burt for him to drop the relationship forever. She also used to encourage me to write a book about my life with Burt. "Maybe he can understand himself better if he reads the truth. He is so out of touch with reality," she said to me on one occasion.

When he needed a designer to do his new restaurant, Backstage, plus a couple of condominiums in South Florida, and his boat, he renewed his friendship with her and she moved to Jupiter with her children, Christine and Rob, who were in their late teens, and Patrick, who was about eight at the time. Patty was an innovative artist in her field of interior design and everything she did for Burt was outstanding.

Once she and I attended the show *A, My Name is Alice* at the theatre and were sitting in Burt's box with Burt and a few of his guests. Donna Pescow was singing "Call Me in the Morning," a song about two girlfriends who kept in touch by phone or over coffee until one of them died. Patty and I cried all through the song. It was about us. We called each other every day and I stopped by her shop for coffee two or three times a week, only for a few minutes, because that's all the time we both had.

Sadly, she was diagnosed with cancer in 1993. I was still in California at the time and she was in Jupiter, Florida. Oddly enough, it was as if we'd switched places.

The last time I spoke with her, she was optimistic as always. "I've got to beat this thing, Elaine . . . and I think I can. Call me in the morning."

She passed away three weeks later, and I'll always miss her.

Nina Blanchard

When we auditioned for the new apprentices each year, Burt called on his friends to assist in judging and selecting the most talented candidates for the next year's class. Charles Nelson Reilly, Lorna Luft, and Nina Blanchard were among the regular judges.

Nina rearranged her schedule and flew in from California to participate. Burt always felt her input was vital, as she has one of the top modeling and talent agencies in the country and had a gift for recognizing real talent. Burt always insisted that we set the date around her schedule, because she not only helped in determining who was right for the program, she returned during the year and taught the kids the correct way to audition. She advised them on their 8 x 10 head shots, supplied them with an enormous amount of information about the industry and counseled them in making their career decisions.

When she came to Florida, Nina stayed at Burt's beach house with Charles Nelson Reilly. She was so fastidious that immediately after she arrived at the house, she ironed all of her clothes so there was not a wrinkle in them. In fact, it was such an issue that on one occasion when she was coming up the driveway in a limousine Nina burst into laughter as the car approached the house. Charles had placed the ironing board and the iron in the driveway to greet her.

I remember one day when Nina, Loni, and I went out for lunch and a day of shopping in Palm Beach. We were in Saks Fifth Avenue, and Loni proceeded to buy some cosmetics. While a salesperson was assisting her, a young girl came up to Nina and me and offered her assistance. Nina decided she needed a tube of lipstick. After the salesgirl had wrapped it, she proceeded to examine Nina's face and discussed at length what products she should use for her skin.

Now, Nina Blanchard has skin like porcelain and has spent her whole life telling young girls what to wear and how to wear it; however, she was very patient with the salesgirl and never let on that she was an expert. Loni and I stood a few yards away and observed, barely able to contain our glee. We waited for over twenty minutes for her to finish before we could go to lunch and have a great laugh about it.

Nina, a few years Burt's senior, once told me that she first met Burt at a dinner engagement arranged by Burt's manager. At dinner she introduced one of her models to Burt, and Nina, who has a great sense of humor, said she committed a faux pas at the very beginning of the evening.

"I really enjoyed your movie *Smokey and the Bear,*" Nina said to Burt.

"I'm really glad to hear that. You might like another one I did called *Smokey and the Bandit,*" Burt retorted.

Nina said she burst out laughing and apologized to Burt, but it was a great icebreaker.

Though strikingly beautiful, the model was a bit of a bimbette, which is one point shy of being a bimbo, and Nina said that Burt, although charming all evening to both of them, appeared to be bored with the model and spent the entire dinner talking with her.

The next day, David Gershenson, Burt's manager, called Nina, whom he had known for many years, and told her that Burt didn't care to see the girl again, but had such a great time talking with Nina that he wanted to take her out.

"Of course I was flattered," Nina told me. "So I said, sure, have him call me."

A short time went by and a call came from David. "I hate to tell you this, but your date with Burt is off. He has fallen head over heels in love with Loni Anderson from *WKRP in Cincinnati* after meeting her on the Merv Griffin show and is going to start dating her."

"C'est la vie," Nina said. "I've had a lot of short-lived romances in my time, but this one set a record!"

Man's Best Friend

Burt loves animals and especially dogs. He had a dog named Bruiser for about sixteen years in Los Angeles. She was part Rhodesian Ridgeback and part Great Dane, she slept on his bed and ruled the Holmby Hills Estate where he lived on Carolwood Drive for many years. When she passed away Burt really missed her companionship and after a short mourning period, he decided to get another dog. He acquired a huge black-and-tan rottweiler and named him Otto.

Otto drooled all over everything in Burt's house and crapped all over the place. Loni hated Otto because he was very affectionate and drooled all over her clothes. Loni gave Burt the BIG ultimatum (one of many), "Either Otto goes, or I go."

Since Burt and Loni were still sleeping together, I guess he decided she was the best bet and shipped Otto off to his ranch. Otto loved the ranch and his new freedom.

After a while, Burt decided he wanted Otto to live on his estate at Valhalla. He wanted him "potty"-trained so that he could stay inside of the house as well, so Burt could enjoy having his dog around him when he was home.

Otto would have no part of Valhalla and he let everyone know it. He left mountainous piles all over the white rugs and urine stains the size of small lakes. It seemed that nothing could be done to improve his manners, as he had become a real "cowdog" who hated city life. They were forced to send him back to the ranch.

"I want to get a dog for Valhalla and I found the perfect one in Kentucky. Please call the lady who owns him and arrange for her to get him to Jupiter." Burt was calling from California. "You'll love him, I named him Sharky and he's a harlequin (black-and-white spots) Great Dane. He's from champion stock, fully trained, and is four years old. I'd like James to take him over to the theatre sometimes, so he'll get used to everybody. He will be sort of the mascot and can just lie around in your office."

Great, Boss, I thought. *I can "doggy-sit," while James runs errands.* I could just picture Sharky and me running up and down the stairs all day between my office and the theatre, and every half hour I'd have to take him outside to "mark his territory" at every bush, tree, and fire hydrant.

I made all the arrangements for the owner and her trainer to drive him down from Kentucky and to stay a couple of days until Sharky became accustomed to his new home and to James, who managed the house and would be taking care of him.

Tommy Ryan, Burt's security manager, James, and I were at the house when he arrived. As he stepped from the station wagon, he was much larger than I had imagined. James, who was just over five feet tall, walked over to Sharky, and I pictured myself saddling the dog up and James riding away into the sunset.

The walkway to the house was all Spanish clay tile, and Sharky would not walk on it.

"Is there another way to get in?" the trainer asked. "He slipped and fell as a puppy on this kind of tile and has been afraid to walk on it ever since."

Tommy, James, and I looked at each other in disbelief . . . the entire downstairs, dining room, living room, foyer, mezzanine, and hallway . . . was Spanish clay tile. There was a rug in the center of the dining room, one in the center of the living room, and a short runner down the hallway to the garage.

It was getting dark and we had to get the dog in the house. We walked around to the back glass doors that entered the dining room, but this dog planted himself firmly. It took three guys to lift him into the dining room and onto the rug. James went to the linen closet and brought back a quilt and placed it connecting the dining-room rug to the glass door. Sharky lay down and there he stayed. No amount of coaxing would get him to step on the tile.

Burt came home a couple of days after we got Sharky. The former owner and trainer had gone back to Kentucky, and James and Sharky had already bonded.

In 1981 during the filming of *The Best Little Whorehouse in Texas,* Burt called me from California to tell me that he, Dolly Parton, Jim Nabors, Charlie Durning, and several others from the film would be coming to Valhalla for the weekend and to have all the guest rooms and dinner prepared for them.

They arrived around eight in the evening and Sharky was on his quilt in the corner of the dining room fast asleep. The front door opened and the lively entourage entered the foyer within sight of the dining room. Sharky sprang to his feet and Burt yelled, "Hey, guys, there's my new dog. Hello, Sharky! Come here, boy!" Sharky just stood still and started to tremble all over. "Here, boy. Come here, boy," Burt called again. "Elaine, what's the matter with this dog? Is he okay?"

"Well, he's just going through a period of adjustment and you guys are pretty loud and startled him out of a deep sleep," I explained.

I had told Burt when Sharky arrived that he was quite timid, but very affectionate when he got to know you; however, I also offered to return him with the owner when she went back to Kentucky if he wished, but he decided to give Sharky a chance.

When Burt walked over to Sharky and patted his head and rubbed his back, Sharky immediately responded. "I guess we did scare you, big guy," he said. "I don't suppose you'll make much of a watchdog, but we still have Tommy."

When everyone sat down at the dining-room table and started eating, Sharky began to relax. He walked from his quilt connected to the dining-room rug and stood by the table at Burt's side. He was so tall, his head and neck towered over the table, and he plopped his head down right next to Burt's plate and stared up at him.

"Honey, it might be a good idea to put him outside while we're having dinner," Burt said.

"Well, Boss," I said, "he won't stay out there because he's afraid of the dark, and besides you folks are really eating in his bedroom."

"What are you telling me?" Burt looked a little concerned.

"Just that he won't go anywhere in the house yet because he's kinda allergic to all this Spanish tile. He once slipped on this kind of tile and broke his leg and now he won't even step on it. However, James and I have it all figured out. We have a lot of those carpet runners upstairs and we'll just move them around until he gets used to the tile," I explained.

"Okay, but for God's sake see if you can find him another place to sleep so my guests don't have to eat in 'his bedroom.' "

Burt really became attached to Sharky and even had him in an opening shot when *Good Morning America* interviewed him in Jupiter. Burt loved to lay out by his pool, and Sharky would settle right at his feet. The pool was not screened in at that time, and was in open view to the boat traffic on the intracoastal waterway. The house was on a slight hill up from the water and people would call from their boats, "Hey, Burt!" whether anyone was outside or not. The local tour boat always pointed out his house as it went up the waterway.

Once a small boat came by carrying two couples on board. They proceeded to dock their boat at Burt's dock while he was sleeping by the pool. As the four of them started walking up the hill toward the house and entered the lawn area, Sharky stood up and barked excitedly. Burt shot up out of his chair in time to see the backsides of two men and two women racing toward the dock as fast as possible. They never noticed that once Sharky had barked so ferociously, he had immediately run around to the back of the house scared to death.

Sharky died of cancer at the age of eight and is buried on the property at Valhalla.

After Sharky's death, I suggested to Burt that maybe it would be better to just get a cat for Valhalla, since he wasn't at home that much any more. I really got so attached to his animals that it was very upsetting to me when they died. Burt agreed. Ironically, a couple of days later, a sleek, black stray cat, who was running from the animal-control unit, jumped a fence and landed on the patio of someone who worked at the theatre, and she was trying to find him a home. I took him over to Valhalla.

Burt and Loni had just returned from Rome, so

he decided to name the cat *Gato,* which is Italian for cat. Gato was absolutely wonderful, but Burt still longed for another dog. "I'd like another harlequin Great Dane like Sharky, so call the lady in Kentucky and see if you can get another one," Burt said.

I was able to obtain a female Dane and when Razzle Dazzle arrived she was absolutely beautiful. She was over a year old, well trained, had beautiful markings, and a great personality. I loved her immediately. Burt was filming *Physical Evidence* and *Switching Channels* during that time, so he was not in Florida as frequently as before and he really didn't get to know her as well as he did Sharky. Unfortunately after James left, we had hired a married couple, who definitely did not work out; another man who had great credentials, but a cocaine problem, so he lasted only a couple of months; and then we hired a slightly built, extremely quiet man, who spoke with a slight accent. He had worked in the United States for some years and we received a good recommendation from his last employer. He had been working for us about a year when Burt decided to get Razzle. He was visibly unhappy about the dog, and he told me that he felt Burt was being inconsiderate of him in asking that he take care of her. I reminded him that Burt was out of town quite a bit and he really had nothing else to keep him busy and that if Burt wanted twelve dogs, it was his job to take care of them.

I began to get concerned when I went to the house and noticed Razzle shying away from the houseman. I was really uneasy about her situation and I wanted to keep a closer eye on her. The houseman called me at the theatre one morning and told me that she was sick and had crapped on the white rug about four times. He was angry about having to clean it up and suggested that Burt should get rid of the dog. She was well trained and always went to the bathroom outside, so I knew she had to be pretty sick and needed attention. The guy could not handle her well enough to take her to the veterinarian's office, so I had him come to Valhalla to take care of her. He tested her for intestinal parasites and everything else, but was unable to determine her problem. Razzle continued to lose weight, was lethargic, and had recurring diarrhea.

The houseman called me one morning and said, "I'm not cleaning up after this damn dog any more. You tell Mr. Reynolds that either she goes or I go. Besides, I put her out in the yard and she is too weak to get up, so you better call that veterinarian."

"If I were you, I wouldn't give Mr. Reynolds that ultimatum. He loves the dog, he doesn't love you."

When I told Burt, he said, "Tell that jerk good-bye."

The guy was furious when I told him to pack his things. He said, "I can't believe he would choose a dog over a human being!"

"He didn't!" I replied.

The houseman had been dating a local girl. When she found out he was fired, she informed us that he had shown her some of Burt's jewelry and one of his guns that he had taken to his apartment, which was located at the end of the driveway over the rehearsal hall. He also went to his safety-deposit box every day, which she felt was suspicious.

I immediately called our security man Tommy Ryan to go with me to the apartment unannounced and confront him. Tommy was so wonderful in these situations. He is the coolest "cop" I've ever known. He can quote the Florida Statutes back and forth, and he handled this guy so well. After talking with the houseman, Tommy walked back into his bedroom with him and returned with one of Burt's guns and a box of jewelry, which included an I.D. bracelet with Burt's name on the front, several rings, and chains. When I called Burt and told him about it, he chose not to press charges against the guy, because anyone who worked as the house manager knew everything that was going on. Burt was afraid of the publicity so the guy was quietly dismissed.

It appeared that there wasn't much left to do for Razzle, so my last husband Lee Hall and I took her to the "little beach house" for a couple of days. It lifted her spirits a bit, because she loved the beach. I had to get up during the night constantly to check on her and give her medication, and she would look up at me with those great big eyes so pitifully and I just held her and cried. One morning she was too weak to stand, so I took her back in to the veterinarian and he told me she was in pretty serious condition.

"Do you think she could have been poisoned?" I asked, knowing how the houseman felt about her.

"I've been trying to determine if that's a possibility, but I'm not having any luck. If she has been, it is something very hard to detect. I'll run some more tests."

Razzle didn't make it, so the vet did an autopsy and sent specimens out to a laboratory in Texas. When the tests came back from the laboratory, the results proved that she had ingested highly toxic chemicals over a period of time. Burt was back in California at the time and when I called him, he was devastated and angry. The S.O.B. houseman had left the state, and to this day, I hope this man experiences a miserably slow death when he goes.

Dolly Parton

When I was in California, I believe it was in October 1981, I was staying at Burt's house on Carolwood Drive in Holmby Hills. Burt was filming *The Best Little Whorehouse in Texas* at Universal Studios. I had come out for a week. Since we had done a production of *Come Blow Your Horn* starring Elliott Gould at Burt's theatre in the early fall and now it was playing in Los Angeles, Burt decided it would be fun to see the west coast production as well. He invited Charles Nelson Reilly, Charles Durning and his wife Mary Anne, and Dolly Parton. He had everybody meet at his house and go to the theatre by limousine. When Dolly arrived at the house, she was wearing a bright red dress with a full skirt and a wide gold belt, which emphasized her ample bosom and tiny waist.

I complimented her when she came into the room and she was very sweet and said to me, "You know, Elaine, I wear these flashy clothes and these big old wigs because the public is used to seeing me this way. They like it and I like to please them."

That night, everyone got into the back of the limousine, but Burt and Dolly decided to ride up front with the driver. The glass partition was open, so we all were able to converse, though we mostly listened to Burt's and Dolly's stories. It was like one big party on wheels.

When we arrived at the theatre, the paparazzi were there, flashing pictures like crazy. To avoid being crushed by anxious fans, we were ushered to our seats minutes before curtain and left as the standing ovation ended. After a short visit backstage, we piled back into the limo.

Charles Nelson Reilly suggested we might enjoy the show at La Cage Aux Folles, a famous Hollywood nightclub where the floor show is comprised of female impersonators. Everyone thought it would be great fun, so we went. The show was hysterical and featured a drop-dead ringer for Ann-Margret. As we returned to the car, the paparazzi were all over the place.

A week later, a picture of Burt and Dolly walking and holding hands was on the front cover of a major tabloid with headlines blazing away about their private, intimate evening out on the town. Dolly was wearing the bright red dress with the wide gold belt, with Mary Anne and Charlie Durning barely visible in the background and the rest of us close behind. Some "private intimate night out on the town"!

A few weeks after I returned to Florida, Burt called from California. "Hi, honey." Burt always called me "honey" as he usually did any other woman around him. It was his Southern upbringing. "Dolly and Jim Nabors and a few others are coming to Florida with me." Burt was calling to tell me that the film *The Best Little Whorehouse in Texas* had wrapped for the weekend and to have James, the house manager, prepare Valhalla for all his guests. Dolly was everything she appears to be on television interviews. She was warm, friendly, gorgeous, and hysterically funny. Burt offered Dolly his room because it had an adjoining ladies' room, and he told me he was going to stay at one of his condos in Jupiter Harbor.

Burt loved to give the "thirty-eight-cent tour" of his ranch, beach house, and theatre. His guests were always treated to whatever play was at the theatre, and they could enjoy dinner and the show in his private box. He really had a great time with his friends and loved to show off the apprentices to the celebrities who were visiting. Many times, if the celebrities were available, they would teach a class. Dolly and Jim were there only for a couple of days, so they entertained the group. We all sat around on the floor in the rehearsal hall while Dolly played the guitar and sang her hit song "Coat of Many Colors." Her performance was so touching that everyone was teary-eyed.

"I love this town, and it is still unspoiled," Burt told his friends. "I think both of you should find a house or condo here on the ocean so you will have a special place to relax." He asked me to arrange to show them a few places in the area. That meant I had to ask the owners to stay away from home for a short while so I could give a private showing.

I remember one house on the ocean had a very grand, marbled-floor foyer, with a semicircular stairway to the second floor. When we reached the landing, Dolly threw her leg over the railing and sang "It's a Little, Bitty Pissant Country Place" from *The Best Little Whorehouse in Texas*.

Jim Nabors was looking for a place on the ocean big enough for his "Mama" and "Aints" (aunts) to enjoy. He is very close to his family and was always thinking of them. It was a lot of fun showing the two of them around, but neither settled on anything. Burt just loved coming home to Jupiter so much, he thought everybody else would feel the same and should own a house there.

Burt talked Universal Pictures into having a Florida premiere of the film. I arranged it with one of the largest movie distributors in Miami and also planned a "By Invitation Only" press reception at Quayside Condominiums, where Burt was given a condo for his use exclusively in return for the use of his name as an occupant. All of the details were carefully planned and fine-tuned. I utilized some of the staff from the theatre including Tommy Ryan to handle security. Approximately three hundred guests arrived, mostly in limos for the reception dressed in their finest. Quayside was right on the edge of the water and required you to enter through a long, narrow drive and circle around the front entrance continuing out the same way. There was no other exit.

The valet parking service had all the limousines lined up in front of the building so the dignitaries could enter them easily and lead the entourage to the theatre for the premiere. Everything went well, and when Burt, Dolly, and the other celebrities left the reception, that was the signal for all to get into their cars for the procession. When I walked out with Burt and Dolly, to my horror, the "head" valet had decided (with the help of the press) to move all of the limos back on the street, so they would drive by the cameras when they picked up the celebrities.

"Where the hell is the car?" Burt asked.

Over there across the street, I realized, and thought, *I'm dead.*

"I guess some idiot decided to move them," I said weakly. Dolly quipped, "Who cares?" and grabbed Burt's hand, "Come on, let's go!" They both grinned and ran across the road. All's well that ends well, you say.

By this time, the reception had pretty well emptied out and most everyone was in their cars and ready to roll. However, two reporters from the local paper—a bit intoxicated from all the free booze— had jumped into their car and drove through the exit of the front entrance, just as the limousines began to enter from the opposite direction creating a traffic jam.

The reporters stopped their car, bumper to bumper with the first limousine, locked their doors refusing to move, and were laughing at the dilemma they had created. The long line of about fifteen limousines, plus all of the cars that had pulled in behind them, bumper to bumper, looked like an Amtrak train.

The local police were trying everything to persuade them to move. Unfortunately, many exuberant theatergoers had pulled out of the parking garage at the same time as the reporters and followed their car, creating another massive traffic jam from the other direction. There was no way to move anyone at that point, other than using a cherry picker from a helicopter to extract the cars one by one and place them on another street. I was out in front begging the police to "please do something!" They maneuvered and jockeyed the cars, after threatening to arrest the reporters if they did not cooperate, and they finally were able to clear the way to begin the motorcade to the theatre.

When we arrived at our destination, thousands of screaming fans surrounded the theatre, with cameras flashing and thrusting pieces of paper out to hopefully get an autograph from the stars. Burt and Dolly were ushered into the manager's office of the theatre until the movie began, so they wouldn't be bombarded with autograph seekers.

This theatre didn't have a taped telephone message and only housed a couple of mini theatres, unlike current theatres which have as many as fourteen or more screens. Whenever the phone rang, Burt and Dolly took turns answering it. The person on the other end of the line would ask what was playing, and Burt or Dolly would give the names of the other two features, but would say, "The best one playing is *The Best Little Whorehouse In Texas*, starring Dolly Parton and Burt Reynolds (depending on who answered the phone and gave the other "top billing"), so you be sure to come and see it. It's sold out tonight, so plan to come tomorrow!" If you told those callers that Burt Reynolds and Dolly Parton had given them the information, they never would have believed it.

The Other Sally in His Life

"Sally lives alone in one of the condos next to the theatre and is in a wheelchair. Her mother just passed away and the two of them used to come to the theatre all the time. Do you know anyone who's looking for an apartment? She has a nice condo and is very self-sufficient. She might like to have company in the house," one of the theatre employees said to me.

"No, I don't, but I'll make a few calls to ask around," I responded. When I met Sally Wagner, she was vibrant, witty, and I must say, for someone confined to a motorized wheelchair with crippling rheumatoid arthritis since she was twelve years old, as mobile as most people who are able to walk.

Sally was able to get to the theatre and surrounding malls and restaurants in the area, so she became well-known all over town. She was always trying to get Vern, our maintenance engineer, to soup up her chair so it would go faster. Extremely bright, and never feeling sorry for herself, she became an inspiration to all who met her.

After Sally met Burt, he opened the doors to the theatre to her, because she had such a great love for it. She had grown up in Washington, D.C., and for many years attended plays at the Kennedy Center with her family. She contributed much time and energy to the kids at the Institute, and Burt always encouraged her to sit in on all the classes he was teaching. He even made her an honorary apprentice.

Burt and Sally spent many hours together. He was intrigued by her intelligence and insight. Whenever he was directing a play at the theatre, Sally always sat next to him, carefully observing his every move. It eventually enabled her to direct scenes with the apprentices, and she is now directing an educational video of a play she wrote called *The Little Pioneer,* the story of Bessie DuBois, a Florida pioneer, for use in the public schools in Palm Beach County. She has also written and produced another two of her original works, *Worth Avenue* and *Katy Star Rider.*

Sally was a constant source of support for anything Burt was involved in, and even spoke up in his behalf at the Jupiter Town Council meetings when he was trying to get approval for building Reynolds Plaza, his office building.

She became president of The Burt Reynolds International Fan Club, a position she still holds and handles all of his fan mail from all over the world.

She also publishes a journal filled with current
pictures and stories to keep his fans up to date on
his activities.

Burt's Fans

"I am Mrs. Burt Reynolds, and I demand to talk to my husband!" the voice screamed into the phone. This fan called at least two or three times a month from somewhere out West and harassed whoever answered the phone. I hated talking to her, but she wouldn't give up until she said what she had to say to me. She always insisted on speaking with me, as I was his secretary at the time.

She'd scream at me, "You are just covering for my husband Burt Reynolds, and I know he's there, so you'd better get him on the phone if you know what's good for you!"

I truly felt sorry for her, but I couldn't take all the phone calls and threats anymore.

When I called Burt's manager at the time, David Gershenson, in California and explained that it was getting very difficult to settle her down, he told me that this particular lady had been making calls to Burt's office in Los Angeles as well for a couple of years.

One day while David was in town, the woman

called and the new receptionist put her through to me. David was in my office and told me exactly what I should say to her, "Burt Reynolds is not married to you or to anyone, he does not know you, nor does he care to know you!"

He then whispered to me, "She's in Nevada, so don't worry, just say it."

I did and she responded, "I know who you are and where you are and I'm sending someone over to take care of you now!"

I asked where she was calling from. She said, "The bus station in West Palm Beach." It was a local call and *she was in town*. My heart stopped and David's only comment was, "Gee, she's never done that before."

The local police were able to track her down and they put her on a bus back to Vegas. But she got off in Stuart, only twenty miles away, caught a taxi, and was back in Jupiter in an hour. She showed up at the theatre, so the manager called the police and I bought her a one-way plane ticket to Vegas. I also sent the theatre's own security person with the local police to drive her to the airport and to make sure she got on the plane.

This "Mrs. Reynolds" was frumpy and at least sixty-five years old. Although she never came back to town, she continued to write demanding and obscene letters and to call on the phone for the next couple of years, demanding to speak to her husband, Burt.

* * *

On another occasion, a determined fan had her best friend dress up like a UPS delivery person and package her up to be delivered to her favorite movie star! When the large box arrived, everyone was very busy and left it unopened. Cramped and hungry after almost a full day, the pretty blonde yelled, screamed, and banged on the sides of the box. Unfortunately, everyone had left the house. She began to panic and clawed her way out of the carton. Fearful that she might get caught by security or possibly worse, Doberman pinschers, she found a phone and called her girlfriend to pick her up. When Burt returned home a week later, he found the torn empty box. He had no clue as to why it was there or what had been inside.

Many years later, while filming *Evening Shade*, he received a note, asking, "May I please meet you now? I don't think I can go through UPS again." Of course he agreed. After that she began attending the filming of the show almost every week!

One night the bar manager in the lobby lounge at the theatre called me at home about midnight. He said a guy who really looked exactly like Burt Reynolds was in the lounge drinking champagne, visiting with the patrons, and signing autographs. He said, "I tried to get him to stop impersonating Mr. Reynolds, but he's so good at it that the patrons think I'm lying."

I got dressed to go over to the theatre and called our security people to meet me there. I must say, he was a dead ringer for Burt and even had the smile and walk down pat. I explained that it was really unfair to represent himself as Burt and that if he offended anyone, Burt would be the one they would be mad at. He was very polite, yet seemed a little strange and kept telling me he was on his way to Boston to buy a lot of clam chowder and was going to send me a case. Our security person escorted him off the property and advised him that he should not return.

We never saw him again until the CIA showed up about three weeks later wanting to know my association with this man. They explained that they arrested him at the White House gate threatening to kill the President. He had no iden- tification on him, only *my* business card that he had picked up at the theatre, and he kept telling them I was his good friend. Oh, yes, I never got the clam chowder.

"Happy Birthday to My Husband," the words on the card addressed to Burt said. It had a local post- mark and inside was written, "I love you so much and miss you terribly. Won't you please come back home?" Greeting cards for all occasions came from this lady—two and three a week for over six months. It was heartbreaking to know someone was hurting so badly. She began to send engraved jewelry, watches, rings, and even a man's wedding band, begging her husband to come back. We were finally able to locate her home address and had Tommy Ryan return everything to her. He said, "I felt so sorry for her. Her husband left her for a younger woman, and I guess she just substituted the Boss for him."

Every day around 4:00 P.M., she would drive to the theatre and sit on the side of the fountain next to the magnificent, bronze, life-sized sculpture of Burt on a bucking bronco. She cried as she sifted through a stack of photographs of Burt Reynolds. When anyone offered to help, she just asked to be left alone. She'd only stay about fifteen minutes. We had security observe "the fountain lady" carefully, but she never bothered anyone. One day the letters stopped and we never heard from her again.

"I feel terrible, I think I have the flu. I'm leaving now for the airport and we should land around five. I'd sure love some chicken soup right now." Burt was calling from his hotel where he was filming *Starting Over.* I stopped at the ranch to pick up one of his cars, because mine was not totally dependable at that time, and Logan Fleming, the ranch manager, said, "Take the Cadillac convertible. We just put a new top on it, so I want Burt to know it's done."

As I was driving about 4:00 P.M. the sun was still shining; however, in South Florida rain is always imminent and about five miles down the Florida

Turnpike, I suddenly drove into a torrential rainstorm making it virtually impossible to see. I turned on the windshield wipers—it didn't help—there was a solid wall of water pouring down between me and the windshield! I thought I had entered the twilight zone. I was drenched, but I couldn't stop laughing. I took the next exit and pulled up into a gas station to use the phone. The rain stopped as quickly as it had begun and I got out of the car soaking wet. I called Logan and he had someone bring me another car, and I continued to the airport dripping wet.

When Burt's private jet arrived, he disembarked wearing a trench coat looking miserable. I drove the car onto the tarmac and up to the steps of the plane. Usually Burt insisted on driving, but he was not feeling up to it. As he crawled into the passenger's seat, he said, "I just want to go home and get into bed. I feel awful."

"Are you hungry?" I asked, "James has some chicken soup for you at the house if you feel like eating."

"I'm really not very hungry and I just want to get some rest," he said.

I looked at his face, which was flushed, and said, "Have you taken your temperature? You look like you have a pretty high fever."

"Earlier during shooting I took some Tylenol and that made me feel a little better, but I haven't had anything since," he said.

"Well, we'll probably skip the soup for now and just get some cool liquids into you and work on getting that fever down," I said as we drove away from the plane.

As we were passing the terminal he said, "Stop the car for a minute." I thought he had forgotten something, but when he rolled down the window I saw a young girl with a camera calling to him. Although he was as sick as a dog, he gave a faint smile and waved, and she got her picture of Burt Reynolds.

He closed his eyes and leaned back in his seat. We drove to the house in silence and I smiled as I thought to myself, *He really does care about his fans.*

I was in the office at Burt's theatre in 1980 sorting through the mail and my phone rang. "Is this Burt Reynolds's secretary?" a sweet, almost tearful voice came over the line.

"Yes, this is Elaine, what can I do for you?" I replied.

"My brother is dying!" she blurted out and began sobbing. My heart instantly went out to her. "He's only nineteen and was in a really bad car accident and has been in a coma for so long my mom and I are afraid he'll never wake up. We have tried everything to connect with him. We talk to him constantly, day and night, and the doctor said to focus on something that was very important in his life at the time of his accident. His room is filled with pictures and magazine articles, and looks like a shrine to Burt Reynolds.

Do you think Mr. Reynolds will write a note to him so we can read it over and over to him? We don't know what else to do!" She began to cry again.

I told her, "I'll say prayers for him and I'll call Burt right now. He's making a movie, but I can reach him." I called Burt and told him about her phone call. He was very moved and sent a letter and a picture with a special inscription to her brother.

Two years later, I received a beautiful bouquet of flowers and a thank-you note from someone named Brian McAlinda. The note said, "I can't thank you enough for what you did for me." I thought, *These flowers are beautiful, but obviously delivered to me by mistake. I'm sure if I had done something to deserve these, I would remember it.*

A few days later, a male voice on the phone said, "I'm Brian McAlinda. My sister called you two years ago when I was in a coma and you got Burt Reynolds to send me a wonderful letter and picture. The first thing I saw when I regained consciousness was Burt Reynolds's picture on my nightstand. It has been a long, hard struggle, but I'm walking, working out, and it's great to be alive!"

He came to the theatre soon after that and when he walked into the lobby, this tall, handsome, twenty-one-year-old man was in awe of everything. "I can't believe I'm really here in his theatre!" he said in a hushed voice. "I just hope someday to meet him personally."

Burt was out of town at the time, but Brian was

so in awe by the theatre and being immersed in those surroundings, that he was happy just to be there. It was sometime later when he finally met Burt face-to-face, and he was able to tell Burt how grateful he was for having "saved" his life.

"I didn't save your life, you did," Burt shyly said.

"When I came to, the first thing I saw was your picture. I can't tell you how much that meant to me."

"Hi, Elaine, remember me?" the voice on the other end of the line said and then announced his name.

"Oh, yes," I responded as I recalled the young man, who was a former employee with a major drug and alcohol problem. "What can I do for you?" I asked.

"I need to talk to Burt about a few things. Is he around? I'm really pissed off at him and I need to straighten him out."

"Well," I continued, "he isn't in town right now, and if it's something you want to discuss with me first, since you know me, maybe I can help you straighten it out."

"No," he said, sounding more irritated and his voice was shaking, "I want to see him personally."

"I'm sorry, but he's not here." I felt a little uneasy as I said goodbye and hung up the phone. He called several more times during the day and with each call he sounded more hostile. I soon became worried and called Mark Baker, who was a detective with the Jupiter Police Department and handled the security for the theatre at that time, just to alert him, as I usually did when I received calls of this nature. Later in the day, I received a call from a staff member downstairs in the theatre. "Elaine, the guy is in the lobby and wants to see you now. I told him you were probably busy."

"No, that's okay, he called earlier, so I'll see what's on his mind," I said.

"I don't think you should right now," he continued, "he's strung out on something weird, trembling all over and really mad!"

"I'll call Mark Baker to meet with us in case there is a problem," I instructed him. "Keep an eye on him, because he probably won't leave until he sees me."

Mark arrived wearing a plain business suit. He seated himself in front of my desk. The upset young man was then ushered upstairs. When he entered my office, he was trembling quite a bit and had a very wrinkled brown paper bag crumpled up under his right arm.

My God, he's got a gun, I instantly thought. He sat in a chair in front of my desk with Mark on his right—between him and the door. I introduced Mark very calmly, explaining that he handled the security for the theatre, and when anyone was angry with Burt, we needed him around to help us resolve the problem. He was a bit irrational, to say the least, and more than just a little frightening. I kept thinking, while he talked in crazy circles, *What the hell am I doing here? I could have stayed in North Carolina twenty years ago, sitting in a rocking chair on the front porch shelling peas and listening to the whippoorwills.*

All at once he screamed, "I'll show you why I hate him!" and jerked the bag from under his arm and started to open it. In a split second Mark had opened his jacket to reveal his shoulder pistol. My heart stopped and all the blood drained from my body.

The guy tore open the bag and instead of a gun, deposited numerous pictures of Burt all torn up. "You see," he screamed, "this is why! Everybody thinks I am Burt Reynolds and that my girlfriend is Loni Anderson."

This man looked as much like Burt Reynolds as I look like Zsa Zsa Gabor. I wanted to scream at him, *Damn you! You scared me half to death because somebody said you look like Burt Reynolds! How would you like to look like Burt Reynolds dead!!* But, of course, I couldn't say anything.

Mark very calmly explained to him that he had no reason to be mad at Burt, and if he came back to the theatre, approached Burt under any circumstances when he was out in public, or visited his home or ranch, that he would be arrested. He settled the guy down and escorted him out of the building, and I went into the ladies' room to throw up.

Burt was alerted so he could keep an eye out for this guy and Mark kept tabs on him and—thank God—the last I heard he moved away.

The Barbie Doll

"This will be a sellout for sure," I thought as rehearsals began for *One Flew Over the Cuckoo's Nest*. It was January 1982, and Burt was directing Martin Sheen, Adrienne Barbeau, and Will Sampson at his theatre in Jupiter, Florida.

Burt was dating a former Miss America and TV anchorwoman, and she was in Florida with him. He was being interviewed on *Good Morning America* at his home in Florida and had introduced me to her. I thought how pretty she was and with her skin so white and the way her black hair was styled, she looked like Snow White.

Burt told me to make sure she stayed in a room with me just a few feet down the hall from where they were filming, because he didn't want the camera to pick her up. During the interview, Burt was asked about his on-again/off-again romance with Sally Field. He took several minutes talking about her being a great actress and how much he still cared for her. She looked at me and said, "Why is he saying all that about Sally? He sounds like he's still in love with her!"

"Burt always talks that way about the former women in his life," I explained, hoping to make her feel better. "You should hear what he says about Dinah Shore. You'd think they were still together."

After the interview, he was very affectionate toward her, and they seemed to be a typically happy couple.

The next morning I was at the rehearsal hall located on his estate at Valhalla and was sitting with a small group of theatre apprentices watching the rehearsal of *One Flew Over the Cuckoo's Nest* directed by her beau, Burt.

Burt called me aside and said, "She is going back to L.A. later this morning, so will you take her to the airport?" I was used to doing this, as Jupiter really had no limousine service at that time, so I asked her for her flight time. For some reason, I felt she really didn't want to leave.

When I mentioned to Burt that her flight required our leaving right away for the airport in order to make it, he said, "You stay right with her and make sure she gets on that plane, because Loni Anderson is arriving this afternoon and Logan is bringing her here to my house. We'll be over at the theatre rehearsing on stage then, so bring her over there. You're going to love her, honey, she looks just like a Barbie doll!" I could tell he was very excited she was coming.

Sensing the urgency of this situation, I rushed,

but she took her time getting everything together. I think we women have that sixth sense whenever someone else is moving into our scene. On our way to the airport she asked me to stop at the drugstore so she could pick up a few items and appeared to do everything possible to delay our trip.

It was *my* responsibility to get her on that plane. I finally "dragged" her into the airport as she threw her full-length mink down on the sidewalk and pulled it into the terminal behind her, à la Hollywood. I had a strong feeling that Burt had given the fur coat to her while she was visiting him. I felt this was another case of Burt giving a "parting" gift to a girlfriend on her way out.

I raced back to Burt's house in Hobe Sound, about forty-five minutes from the airport, and told James Torrie to help me go through Burt's bed linens, the drawers in the nightstands, dresser drawers, and to check both bathrooms to eradicate any possible evidence of another woman. Sure enough, under the pillows on both sides of the bed, she left sweet little love notes to Burt.

I had never met Loni before and this was the first time she had come to Jupiter. She arrived later that day in Burt's A-Star helicopter and landed on the dock in front of his house. I said to James, "Burt's right, she does look like a Barbie doll." She really was quite beautiful.

After she had freshened up, I drove her the few miles to the theatre where Burt was busy directing. When she walked in, everything stopped. He came over and kissed her very gently and said, "God, you're gorgeous!"

I looked at the two of them together and thought, *Barbie and Ken . . . alive and well in Jupiter, Florida!*

Although my official title was executive director of the Burt Reynolds Dinner Theatre, Burt still relied on me at that time to handle his personal business and entertain his out-of-town guests as well. The next day, he asked me to take Loni shopping and to lunch. I really liked her and she and I shared several mother/daughter stories. Her daughter Deidre was a few years younger than my Lori, who was twenty at the time. I remember we discussed past marriages for both of us and—being working, single parents—how lucky we both were to have had our mothers available to help care for our children.

As we shopped and she tried on her size 4s, I thought, *In my next life, I want to come back with that face and body!*

Throughout the years that I worked for Burt, Loni and I really had many fun times shopping; of course, it was a great break for me because I rarely ever had time to shop for myself. Before Quinton was adopted, we never had a bodyguard and could walk freely in the malls and in Palm Beach.

One of our favorite lunch spots was Cafe L'Europe in Palm Beach. It was always interesting to watch the change in demeanor with the maitre d' when I was with Loni. He would make a gallant hand gesture and greet us with a warmly formal, "Right this way, please, Miss Anderson."

Although people used to follow along behind us in small groups, they usually did not approach us. Once I jokingly told her, "Don't get nervous, this happens every time I go shopping. I just seem to attract all these people." She just laughed and said, "They're very good about not bothering us, aren't they?"

Sometimes a fan would get enough nerve to come up to her and say, "You are much prettier in real life than on television."

Once I commented to an older lady when she said that and I was standing next to her, "Oh, we're actually twins. I just don't bleach my hair."

The lady smiled sweetly and said, "Oh, you're very pretty, too, dear." We both got such a laugh.

In the first couple of years of her relationship with Burt, they both seemed very happy. She really loved the life she had in Los Angeles, but when she came to Jupiter, it was boring for her and Burt spent most of his time either at the theatre or his ranch. There was nothing for her to do but go shopping or occasionally to lunch. She really did not have any special friends there, so Burt would give me a day off now and then to entertain her. Of course, I always had my mobile phone with me and usually would get several calls from him or the theatre.

I remember one day Loni called and said, "Burt is treating us to a day at Mira Linder's (a salon for hair, facials, makeup, manicures, massages, and the works) today, so come pick me up at 9:30." I was thrilled. During the course of the "treat from

Burt" I counted exactly twelve phone calls from the theatre and Burt. On the way back to Burt's house Loni smiled and said, "Now wasn't that a lovely treat. I'm so relaxed, aren't you?" Oh, yes, I was relaxed all right. I had jotted down three major problems to deal with at the theatre and had a list a mile long of things to do for Burt when I got back, but my manicure looked great.

Burt really wasn't crazy about going out to dinner, but Loni was so bored in Jupiter that it was something to do to amuse her. He often invited me and my then husband Lee to go with them and usually we went to The Backstage, his restaurant in Jupiter that was decorated in a thirties theme and was noted for its great jazz artists.

Loni seemed to aggravate Burt in the most subtle ways. She knew which buttons to push and when. One night we were having dinner in a beautiful French restaurant, everyone was in a great mood, and we were all having fun. The waiter came to our table and with a most exaggerated, phony French accent delivered a description of the dinner fare for the evening. When he left the table, Burt said, "If you wake him up in the middle of the night, he doesn't talk like that."

We all laughed and when he came back, he reviewed the special dishes again. On one particular dish we all said, "That sounds great!"

"Okay," Burt said, "go no further, we don't even need a menu, we'll all have that!"

"I want a menu," said Loni. "I might see something better."

"Damnit! She always does that to me," he said. "She loves to embarrass me."

Lee smiled and said, "I know what you mean. Elaine always does that to me, too." I wanted to clobber him. He always agreed with everything Burt said.

Loni managed to get Burt angry about something all the time. She would drop a little bomb and he'd explode, and she would just get a little pouty look on her face and say, "Darling, I don't know what you're so upset about," which set him off more. She would then get very quiet and look around as if she were all alone.

Burt's Business

"What the hell is Burt doing buying 'chicken stores'?" his attorney in Jupiter asked me one morning in his office.

"Oh, you mean the Po' Folks restaurants?" I asked. "Well, his business manager seems to think it's a good investment."

"Well, I don't think so at this time, and I can't seem to get through to him," his attorney continued.

Bill Morrison sat in his office on the fourth floor of Reynolds Plaza and shook his head. "He has The Backstage restaurant downstairs and that should be enough. I think it's a big mistake for him to become involved."

"Well, you know Burt, if it's something he wants to do, nobody can change his mind," I said. Unfortunately, Burt should have listened to Morrison, because he lost millions investing in those restaurants.

When Burt still had the seven Po' Folks restaurants in South Florida and most of them had already closed costing him millions of dollars, he decided to change the name of the one located in West Palm Beach to Ol Bud's. Well, he was soon slapped with a lawsuit by the owners of Bud's Take Out Chicken, a longtime successful chain of fried chicken restaurants in Palm Beach County, for infringing on their name and confusing the public into thinking they were the same company. The prosecuting side was saying that Burt's nickname was "Buddy" Reynolds, not "Bud," and I had to go to court on Burt's behalf and verify that Burt's mom, dad, sister, and brother called him "Bud" all the time and their children called him "Uncle Bud." It got him off the hook. After the aggravation and negative publicity, Burt brought in a restaurant consultant who talked him into changing the name to Daisy's Diner, but the restaurant failed anyway.

"I want you to go down to Ft. Lauderdale with me. I've got another restaurant and it's going to be beautiful," Burt said, sounding so excited. We landed Burt's helicopter on the dock at the Port Authority where all the big cargo ships dock. Way out at the very point of the peninsula, was a beautiful Mediterranean-style restaurant.

"How do you get to this place, by helicopter or boat?" I asked.

"Well, it seems a little difficult, but when you come through the guard gate at the front of the Port Authority, there will be signs directing you around," he answered.

Oh God, I thought. *This is one of Burt's investments that will never make it.* I was wrong.

Jack Jackson, blond, handsome, and always wearing a fabulous smile, was the owner with an excellent track record in successful restauranteuring. Burt's participation was to lend his name and celebrity status to enhance the marketing of the restaurant. Jack's beautiful wife, Cathy, graciously greeted patrons and supervised many of the special events held at the restaurant.

The grand opening of the restaurant was carefully planned and Burt chartered two private planes to bring all of his celebrity friends over for the gala event. The restaurant is located directly across the waterway from the Pier 66 hotel where Burt's friends were housed. The afternoon of the event was a beautiful, sunny day, and the place was packed with dignitaries from all over Florida. Hoards of spectators all gathered outside of the restaurant, hoping to get a glimpse of some of the celebrities.

The stars were brought over to the restaurant from Pier 66 on a huge yacht. Ricardo and Georgianna Montalban, Bob and Heather Urich, Ernest and Tova Borgnine, and Henry Silva were only a few who approached me and asked where they were to go. These folks were used to coming to Burt's theatre or home and depending on me to play hostess and direct them. However, all arrangements were made for the celebrities by David Gershenson, so this was neither my party nor my territory, and I didn't have a clue. I finally found someone who could tell me where the private dining room was, and as I turned to Ricardo and motioned for him to follow me, all of the other celebrities fell into line.

It was a wonderfully festive occasion and guaranteed the success of Burt's new venture. Everyone who was anyone in Florida was there that evening except Burt. He had experienced a kidney-stone attack back at the hotel, so he never made it to the restaurant. He had laser surgery the next day to take care of the stone.

Burt has always been sensitive to the press. *The Palm Beach Post* once carried a large cartoon on the editorial page depicting an exaggerated group of businesses with Burt's name attached, including Burt's Bar-B-Q, Burt's Used Cars, Burt's Burgers, and several others. When he saw it, he really got upset and decided to drop his name from the dinner Theatre and call it The Jupiter Theatre. We had heated discussions and tried to make him realize what a mistake it would be from a marketing and financial standpoint, because everyone would think he was no longer connected with the theatre. "But, Boss," I argued, "people come from miles away just to have their picture taken next to the sign with your name! It won't be the same to them!" He finally consented to allow his name to stay if the size was reduced and a new logo with Jupiter Theatre in much larger letters was created. Understand, this was a great expense, because the logo had to be changed on everything connected to the theatre.

Once a theatre reviewer mentioned that the entrance into the lobby looked like a shrine to Burt Reynolds with all the souvenir T-shirts, ashtrays, pictures, carry-all bags, etc. How the heck Burt got a copy, I don't know. I tried to keep things of this nature from him, because he would make emotional decisions instead of good business decisions. He insisted that I have the gift shop moved to the back of the lobby instead of the front entryway. I argued that the revenue loss would be great and that a lot of people, who are waiting to purchase tickets, would not see it in the back. Nevertheless, he insisted I have it moved . . . another expense, plus we lost $34,000 in revenue the next year. This convinced him to allow me to move it back to the front of the lobby at an additional expense.

The theatre had never been financially stable. With a 450-seat house and the huge production costs, it was impossible to just break even. It was Burt's theatre and if he wanted to do a certain play at a particular time, we had no choice. We ran musicals for six to eight weeks and straight plays for four weeks. We were open year-round and existed on presold subscriptions.

An example of the kind of losses we encountered was when we produced *The King and I* in September 1987. The budget for costumes alone was extremely high and the production costs were way out of line, but Burt insisted on presenting a top quality production no matter what the price.

Yul Brynner had passed away not long before and we cast his understudy from the Broadway production. This actor, not wanting to be compared to Brynner, chose to portray the king much too softly. The show got bad reviews, sales were off, and we lost $250,000.

I worked very closely with each of his business managers and made sure they received any records and explanations of Burt's expenditures, and even had to disclose confidential information regarding expensive personal gifts purchased for his girl-friends other than "business" gifts that were hidden under "acceptable" names, usually that of family members.

Burt really never wanted to be bothered with the day-to-day accounting of his business, so everything usually was directed through Lamar Jackson and me. We tried to keep him abreast of his and Loni's credit card bills and cash, but it was hard to do because neither of them wanted to hear about it. Every dollar was allotted to something before he even made it. Once Loni called me in tears, "Gelson's (supermarket) has cut off our credit, we have no food! Also I was so embarrassed today while shopping in Neiman-Marcus because Burt's Visa card was not accepted."

The credit cutoff at Gelson's Market was one of many. Burt's former business manager used to send me the invoices he was going to pay. I always insisted, and had Burt to back me up, that all the cleaners, yard maintenance, family-owned mailbox stores, picture framers, and any small business had to have priority for payment. I hated to walk in some place and have the owner or his wife say, "We know Burt is having a hard time, so we still honor his orders, yet we need some of the back money paid in order to keep going ourselves."

Unfortunately, no one could ever maintain any control over their own expenditures—especially Burt and Loni themselves.

"I've Got the First Lady
on Hold!"

Quite often when Burt wanted to woo a particular actor or actress to appear at his theatre or with him in a movie, he would arrange a meeting and I had to become his accomplice.

"I need you to do me a favor tonight," said Burt. "Julie Walters, who did the movie *Educating Rita* is having dinner with me in my box tonight. Her manager is with her, so I want you to join us for dinner. I need you to get her manager out of the room for a while so I can try to talk Julie into doing my next movie. Her manager is a tough broad and she doesn't want Julie to do the film. I need you to have dinner with us and at some point, get the manager out of the room, so I can talk with Julie alone."

"Okay, Boss, at some point I'll start talking about our setup in the theatre downstairs and invite her to go with me on tour," I responded.

Once the stage was set, Julie and her manager

arrived, and we began with champagne, table-side preparation of dinner—the works!

During the meal, one of my staff came into the box and quietly said to me, "There's a call from Mrs. Reagan for Mr. Reynolds."

"You take it, honey. It might just be a crank call," Burt said.

The call was legitimate, so I apologized for the delay, put the call on "hold," and went back into the box.

"It's the First Lady, Boss, shall I tell her you're not here?" I joked.

He picked up on the joke and answered, "God, is Nancy calling again? She just won't leave me alone. Tell her I'll call her back . . . soon!"

"Well, I hope you will this time," I continued. "She misses you so much and Ronnie is off somewhere and she's so lonely!"

I went back and explained that he would call her back as soon as he was out of his meeting.

I knew he had only a short time to set this deal with Julie before the show started, so I had to work fast to get the manager out of the picture.

I discussed all the special things Burt had done at the theatre and suggested "they" walk downstairs to look around. As they started to rise, Burt looked at Julie and said, "Wait for a minute with me until I finish my story." He turned to me and said, "You girls go on downstairs and we'll be right down."

I knew that now Burt could begin his strategy to entice Julie to costar in his film.

Her manager walked over to the gift shop and said, "He certainly is an egotistical bastard, isn't he? Look at all these T-shirts with 'I Spent The Night With Burt Reynolds' on the front of them."

"Yes, but it says 'At The Burt Reynolds Dinner Theatre' on the back. Besides, this is one of our biggest sellers. Women buy them for themselves, their daughters, sisters, friends, and anyone else who is female. Men buy them for their wives, girlfriends, daughters, sisters, mothers, and everybody else as well."

As we continued to browse, she looked up at me with a startled expression, "Christ! Those two are up there alone together and he's probably trying to talk her into doing a film. I don't want her to go commit to anything unless I'm there!" She turned abruptly and raced upstairs, with me right behind.

As we entered Burt's box, he looked up and grinned, "Hi, girls!"

"You're pretty sly. You tried to pull a fast one," she said to Burt and turned to Julie. "You didn't stick your neck out, did you?"

"No, I didn't—even though it was a charming offer," she said and smiled at Burt.

After they left I said to Burt, "Sorry I couldn't keep her any longer, she caught on too fast."

"It's okay. Julie was pretty up front and said she just couldn't commit. I really like her though and I'd love to work with her," he said.

I reminded Burt of the First Lady's call and since she was calling from their ranch in California and it was three hours earlier on the West coast, he called her back. Even though Burt and I had joked about their relationship, he and Nancy had a very special friendship.

Sex, Drugs, & TMJ

Burt's prescription drug use became a serious problem during the filming of *Stick* in 1985. He was taking an enormous volume of prescribed drugs at that time. He was under a lot of stress with the film, as well as suffering an extremely painful bout with a temporomandibular joint (TMJ) disorder, brought on by a blow to the jaw during a fight scene in a movie he made several years before. I have observed him on many occasions open a prescription bottle and pour ten to twelve pills into his hand and swallow them.

"My God, Boss, how many of those did you take?" I'd ask and this question always seemed to set him off.

"Damn it, I'm not abusing them," he would insist. He was always on the defensive when I questioned him about his use of any prescription drugs. "The doctor said I could take a couple or so if I needed to." Burt always seemed to think that if one or two would help, four or five would work twice as well. He took large quantities of Percodan and Valium, as well as Halcion at night to sleep.

He could usually depend on certain "friends," plus there were always one or two crew members on the set wherever he was working, who would provide him with the prescription drugs he wanted. They would simply make an appointment with their own personal doctor, request the pills for themselves, and with great pride, "help Burt out." In their minds they were supposedly locking in their position close to "the Emperor's ear." Burt usually told these people that he was relying on them because he had left his prescriptions at home and his local doctor would not prescribe the medication without an exam he didn't have time to schedule.

I often wondered if these same people ever stopped to think that their employment depended on Burt's ability to work. I guess that to them it was more important to be in the "inner circle" for the moment than to worry about his health. It was pretty obvious to anyone who was around him for any length of time that he had a serious substance-dependency problem. I can honestly say that I never filled a prescription in my name for him. Although I refused many times, he never pressured me to do so. . . . He didn't need to, there were so many others.

Back in the early eighties, Burt had an interview scheduled with Tom Brokaw at his home in Jupiter. Burt had converted a four-car garage under the maid's quarters into a rehearsal hall, so he could occasionally schedule play rehearsals at his convenience rather than going to the theatre. The television crew arrived on time to set up all of the cameras and lights as scheduled. However, when Tom was ready to begin, Burt was nowhere in sight. He kept everyone waiting almost an hour. To stall for time I talked with Tom, filling him in with information I felt would be helpful regarding Burt's love for his theatre and the apprentice program for young actors he had established there. Tom was truly a gentleman and did not appear to be agitated, even though he and his crew were kept waiting.

Finally when Burt came through the door, I knew he had obviously taken something, because he was talking in a very loud and boisterous manner. Normally he was rather quiet and a little nervous before an interview. When Tom sat down with him in the preinterview he asked several questions about the theatre and the apprentice program, but Burt appeared to be a bit giddy as though he had forgotten the question. Tom held his course, trying to keep some semblance of order in the conversation.

At one point, Tom asked him, "Now, what does Elaine do?" Burt's answer startled and embarrassed me. "Well, Elaine does everything! Why, she'll probably go to bed with the cameraman," he laughed.

I nearly dropped my teeth when he said that. Visibly upset I marched up to him and said, "How could you say a thing like that! I've never done anything like that and you know it!"

He just laughed and said, "I was just kidding, for Christ's sake."

"Well, I don't think it's funny and I'm sure Christ wouldn't either!" I said. I was too embarrassed to face Tom or anyone in the crew after that, so I left him to do the interview alone, thinking, *Go ahead and act like a jackass, I'm not going to stay around and cover for you.* When I told him about it later, he never remembered saying it. With careful editing at the network, the interview was at least acceptable, and I'm sure the public probably thought he was wonderful.

All the rumors that Burt had AIDS started in mid-1985, when I assisted in putting him in the hospital in Jupiter, Florida. Dr. Harry Demopoulas had flown in from New York to assist in helping Burt get over his dependency on prescription drugs.

After a couple of days of treating Burt, he explained to me that he was putting Burt on a strict diet and a regimen of multivitamins to help support his reduction of Burt's intake of the many drugs he was on. He explained to me that Burt's TMJ problem and the resulting pain was so severe that he could not be taken off all drugs until the problem was corrected. He also told me that Burt would be experiencing some definite withdrawal symptoms, but should be all right.

I had spoken to his TMJ doctor, Dr. Gus Swab, in San Diego earlier in the day because Burt had accidentally stepped on his dental retainer and applied a liberal amount of super glue and put it back in his mouth.

Dr. Swab told me to get it from him and throw it away, because it could cause more damage. When Dr. Demopoulas left to go back to New York that day, I received a call from our security chief Tom Ryan. Tommy informed me that I needed to come to the house immediately because Burt was in trouble.

When I arrived, Burt was sitting in a wing-backed chair and appeared to be semiconscious. I kept saying, "Boss, can you hear me?" He didn't respond. I prayed, "God, please don't let him die." Frantically I called the paramedics and asked that they not use the siren coming into the long, winding driveway to the house. There was no one at the house except Tommy, the houseman, and me. The paramedic examined Burt and said to me, "We have to give him a shot of morphine immediately. He is in extreme pain!"

I said, "No! He's allergic to everything and he might die!" I was still urgently trying to reach his TMJ doctor in San Diego, plus Dr. Demopoulas was still in flight. Unable to reach either one of them, I called my own personal physician, Dr. Nicholas Petkas, who immediately came over. After examining him, Dr. Petkas said, "It's a good thing you didn't let the paramedic give him the morphine, it could have killed him. Since we do not know what medication is in his system, and he has definite withdrawal symptoms, he needs to be hospitalized."

Anytime there was a possibility of any publicity relating to Burt's personal life or career, I immediately called David Gershenson, to inform him. When I explained what was happening, David said, "You can't put him in the hospital! The press will eat him alive!"

"Well," I said, "they may eat him *dead* if he stays here, and since I'm here with the body, I'm putting him in the hospital." I hung up the phone, just as the whir of the helicopter blades came over the house and landed on the dock.

Loni Anderson swept into the house wearing a dazzling minidress and asked what was going on. When I explained what had happened, she ran over to Burt and said, "It's okay, honey, I'm here now." He was still so out of it that he didn't respond.

I explained that we were taking him to the local hospital and she said, "Oh, no. We can't do that because of the press!"

I thought to myself, *Good Lord, is that why so many actors die?* I've heard of the power of the press, but this is scary! When the doctor finally convinced her it was vital for him to go, she announced, "Well, I'm going with him to the hospital."

I explained that we were registering him under an assumed name to try and keep down the publicity. Ever the actress, she said she would go upstairs and put on a disguise to avoid being recognized. In a few minutes, she came downstairs wearing tight jeans, a top showing off her bountiful breasts, her hair up in a cowboy hat, and dark glasses. Dr. Petkas took one look at her and said, "Where are the flashing neon lights? We'll have to take you through the morgue if no one is to recognize you!"

We slipped him into the hospital under the name of one of his former hairdressers, and he was immediately put into the Intensive Care Unit. Two specialists were called in—a doctor of internal medicine and a neurologist—who examined him and determined he should remain several days for treatment. They conferred with Dr. Demopoulas in New York and Dr. Swab in California to determine what drugs had been administered, and I also gave them the name of another doctor in Los Angeles, who frequently prescribed Halcion, Percodan, and Valium to him, because I had found numerous prescription bottles in his bathroom. All of the doctors agreed that if Burt did not go into a drug rehab program, he was on the road to certain death.

A few days later, Burt called me from the Jupiter Hospital at 6:00 A.M. announcing, "I'm busting out of here, so come pick me up."

"Boss," I said, "the doctors have to release you before you can leave and it's six A.M."

"I'm not waiting for them, come get me or I'm calling a cab," he said and I knew that he meant it.

"Okay, okay, I'll call Tommy and he'll come pick you up." I frantically called the phone numbers I had for his doctors and left a message. One of them called me right back. "Please release Burt, or he'll leave anyway," I pleaded and he agreed to comply.

Next I called his house to alert Loni that he was on his way home. "What!!" she exclaimed on the other end of the phone. "I thought he was supposed to be in the hospital at least a week, so I invited Deidre (her daughter) and Linda (her manager) to come and stay with me. They just got in last night. What am I supposed to do now? I can't put them into a hotel. I know he doesn't like Linda, but what about me?" She started to cry.

I called Burt to ask what he wanted to do and he yelled, "What the hell did she bring them out here for! She knows I can't stand Linda and besides, what about me! I almost died and she's inviting people to my house to keep 'her' company!"

I had already given some thought to his possible reaction. "Boss, what if I suggest they move to the beach house. They'll be right on the ocean, they'll have a pool, and Loni can go over and visit."

"I don't care where you put them, just get them out of there!" he yelled.

I went over to the house and talked again with Loni and Linda, then helped them pack and move into the beach house. Burt came home and went straight to bed. The next afternoon, I left the theatre and went over to the house to see him. Loni was downstairs and she had been crying.

"What happened?" I asked.

"I'm just so torn," Loni confessed to me. "Deidre is upset with me because I haven't spent enough time with her, and Burt is upset because he feels I should be here to look after him. I just don't know what to do."

I took a deep breath and composed my thoughts. Finally I answered, "Go upstairs and tell him that I am here now and that I suggested you go over and spend the evening with Deidre and have dinner and some mom time, and I'll settle here in the living room and watch television. If he needs anything, I'll be here."

With that she went upstairs, and in a few minutes, Burt came down and said to me, "Loni said you'd stay so she could have dinner with Deidre. I didn't mean to be such a jerk, but I'm going through so much right now, and I didn't need this."

"I know, Boss, but I'll be here if you need me."

Burt went back up to bed and Loni came downstairs, kissed me on the cheek, and said, "Thanks so much. I won't be too long."

Shortly after Burt had been released from the Jupiter Hospital, he appeared on the cover of a major tabloid shown with Tommy Ryan helping him into the car, with the horror story of "Burt Reynolds Hospitalized With AIDS" blazed across the headlines.

I thought to myself, *My God, he's lost so much weight, because the pain in his jaw from the TMJ keeps him from eating and everyone who reads it will believe it's true.* The rumors lasted for several years and Burt was both devastated and angry by the damage this false rumor caused to his career . . . and to his pride. To this day, he still gets upset when the story is mentioned.

After his release from the hospital, he flew back to California with Loni and entered a drug rehab program. He stayed clean for a while and during this time, I would start to discuss something with him that we had shared and he'd have a blank stare on his face.

"I guess that happened when I was asleep," he'd say.

The Green-eyed Monster

Throughout their relationship, Burt and Loni had frequent lover's spats. During one of these times, Loni was in Hawaii, and Burt and Sally got back together. They went to his theatre one night and it was reported in one of the tabloids that "he used his key to a private entrance and they watched the show from his private box." The reunion did not go as well as expected, so after Sally left Burt had me call Loni and tell her the article in the tabloid was not true. And, it wasn't. Burt did not have a private entrance to his box, and he never had a key to anything in the theatre.

It was the manager's job to always be prepared for him and have everything open. Loni was not very receptive of the story, but resolved to drop the issue. A couple of days later, I received a beautiful orchid plant from Hawaii. Loni had enclosed a sweet note and I placed the plant on my kitchen counter.

When Loni came back from Hawaii, she immediately came to Valhalla. James and I had put the

Sally Field pictures and her little ceramic frogs away and replaced them with Loni pictures and her memorabilia. Burt came home for the weekend from Ft. Lauderdale, Florida, where he was filming *Stick* and settled in with Loni I must say she kept her cool pretty well while she was with him; however, after a couple of days, my phone rang.

"Elaine, this is Loni," the voice said on the phone. I had just finished dinner and was relaxing at home. "I just had to talk to you," she continued, "I am so upset, because James just told me that Sally Field was here in the house while I was away."

"What?!!" I responded with the mock astonishment my job demanded. "Loni, that's crazy. Why would James tell you that? That's not like him at all. What's going on over there?"

"I tricked him into telling me. I told him that Burt had already admitted to me that she was here with him, and then I said, 'It must have been very difficult for Sally to get up the stairs since her leg was in a cast!'" She was referring to the fact that Sally had been in a hot-air balloon accident and had fractured her leg a few weeks before.

As Loni continued talking my "watch out for the trap" antenna went up instinctively. "James then said to me, 'Oh, it took a little while, but she managed.' Elaine, I just can't believe Burt would do this. I suspected, but I need to know. James is telling the truth, isn't he?"

Weighing my words carefully, I said to her, "Loni, you know my first loyalty is to Burt, why would you ask me? Even if it was true, I wouldn't say. If you really want to know, ask Burt, not me."

"He and I are driving back to Ft. Lauderdale to the set tomorrow morning and I don't want to upset him, so I can't bring it up. I just need to know if it is true, so I can deal with it myself," Loni said.

I knew her well enough at that point to know that she would definitely bring it up on the way to Ft. Lauderdale. "If you want to know the truth, Loni, you'll have to ask Burt, not me," I said. When I hung up, I called James immediately. He was shocked that she had called me.

"I don't understand," James said, "she was so convincingly sweet about Burt telling her that Sally stayed here and that their relationship was all over. She seemed not to be concerned at all and was very forgiving."

"She tricked you, James," I responded. "Remember, she's an actress. You know I have to call Burt and tell him about this so he'll be prepared. If you wish to tell him yourself, please do."

"No, I think it's better for you to do it. He's going to go crazy anyway, and you can handle him better than I," James said quietly. "I guess I'll lose my job over this."

"I surely hope not," I told him before we hung up.

When I told Burt about the call from Loni, he was in another part of the house away from her. He started to yell, and I told him, "Boss, she tricked James. He has never disclosed anything before. I know it was a dumb thing to do, but she is very cunning. James is devastated and truly sorry."

"I don't care how sorry he is!" Burt insisted. "He works for me and is too close to everything in my life. I don't feel I can ever trust him again, so you have to let him go!"

I was devastated. "Boss," I said, "maybe she won't bring it up in the car tomorrow, since you've told her it is over with Sally, maybe she'll let it pass, or just hit you with it at a later time."

"Well," he said, "I'm certainly not going to bring it up to her, but she'll never let it pass. You'll have to get rid of James while I'm in Lauderdale." Burt and Loni left the next morning as planned, acting as if nothing had happened. He called me later that day.

"Well, she waited until we were about a half hour out of Lauderdale and then told me. She said that she had tricked you into telling her that Sally stayed at the house and you told her Sally had a tough time climbing the stairs."

"What?!!" I screamed into the phone. But before I could say anything else, he said, "Hold it! I yelled at her and said, 'Elaine would never tell you anything like that. I know you're lying.' I must have scared her because she immediately said, 'No, it was James, I told you Elaine because I felt you wouldn't fire her and you might fire James, and besides I tricked him into telling me.' Honey, I hate to lose him, but you'll have to tell James today, and that's final. Start looking for someone else."

I hung up the phone and began to cry. James

was a Scotsman, who was about 5'5" tall and
smoked a pipe. He was such an honorable man
who always genuinely cared about Burt throughout
the years he worked for him. Everyone who worked
at the theatre loved James. He had a wonderfully
dry wit and was always willing to do anything for
anyone. I had no choice but to fire James as I had
been ordered. It was a sad day when he left, and
I especially resented the fact that it was Loni who
was responsible for his termination.

Ironically, several years later Loni told me that
she had been involved with a guy in Hawaii during
the time Burt and Sally were together in Jupiter.
So, I guess what's good for the goose, is good for
the gander!

Bon Air Beach House

"I want to buy this little house. It's right on the beach and the price is right," Burt said as we left the little two-story house on the northern end of Jupiter Island called Bon Air Beach.

"Well, the lot is small and there is no way to secure it. Are you planning to use it sometimes?" I asked.

"It will be fun eventually to decorate it myself, and we can use it for a guest house when some of my friends come in from California or are appearing at the theatre," he said.

He bought the little house for under $300,000, which eventually replaced the big beach house on the southern end of Jupiter Island when his financial situation required him to sell that one. The price included all the furnishings so Burt just brought in a lot of his pictures and a few mementos to "freshen" it up.

One night while at the theatre, Burt and Loni were entertaining some friends in his private box and Loni turned to me. "I saw your new house today. Burt flew me over in the helicopter and said, 'I bought that little house for Elaine.' "

"Excuse me?" I said. It was in the mid-eighties and I was in the midst of a divorce at the time. I was renting one of Burt's condos in Jupiter Harbour in the building next door to mine until my divorce was final and I could move back into my own place. Jupiter Harbour was a five-minute drive to my office at the theatre. I had lived there for five years and really didn't want to move. The Bon Air house was a good twenty-five minute drive to work and was very secluded.

"You must have misunderstood him. He bought that as an investment and to use for a guest house for his friends appearing at the theatre," I explained to Loni.

"No," Burt said, "I wanted to surprise you. I think you should live there. You love the beach so much and it's a great place to get away from all the stress at the theatre. So you can move in whenever you like."

I must admit, I felt a little embarrassed as everyone in the box turned and looked at me, so I had to say something.

"I don't know what to say . . . thank you. I do love the ocean so much and the sea turtles come up on the beach to lay their eggs there. It will be very restful." *And scary living by myself,* I thought.

The next day I thanked Burt again, but told him I would much rather stay in Jupiter Harbour. He was so insistent that I move into the house that I began to feel guilty so I said, "I'll move in, but I'll

Burt and me, 1992.   (*Copyright © 1994 by Lisa Smith*)

(*Left to right*) Mr. and Mrs. James Brolin, Dinah Shore, "Miss September," Burt, Jim and Carole Hampton in 1973 when Burt decided to go into the horse racing business and almost lost his shirt.

Sally Field, Burt and friends at the ranch in 1979. "They always looked so cute together." (*Copyright © 1994 by Jim Deacy*)

Looking great as usual even without makeup, Sally was not too crazy about having her picture taken in the backyard of Burt's parents' home at the ranch.
(*Copyright © 1994 by Jim Deacy*)

BR Ranch, Burt's 160 acre spread in Jupiter, Florida that he called home. *(Copyright © 1994 by Jim Deacy)*

The Burt Reynolds Dinner Theatre was Burt's dream come true. We lost money, but we were proud of the Broadway quality shows we did. *(Copyright © 1994 by Jim Deacy)*

Burt and Sally in *The Rainmaker* in February, 1979 at Burt's theatre. (*Copyright © 1994 by Jim Deacy*)

Burt and me backstage after he played Starbuck in *The Rainmaker*—exhausted but happy. (*Copyright © 1994 by Jim Deacy*)

Tammy Wynette in concert at Burt's theatre. "She stood by
her man...but he had another woman standing by."
(*Copyright © 1994 by Jim Deacy*)

Burt was always nervous about performing on his own
stage because he had an ongoing battle with the local
drama critics. He was terrific when he starred with Carol
Burnett in *Same Time Next Year* in January, 1980.
(*Copyright © 1994 by Jim Deacy*)

In 1980, Liz Taylor visited Burt and attended our production of *Babes in Arms.* But the best show was in Burt's private box.   (*Copyright © 1994 by Jim Deacy*)

Dinah taped her show at Burt's theatre in 1980. She had a lot of fun with Carol and Burt. (*Copyright © 1994 by Jim Deacy*)

When Dinah and Burt were together on stage, their deep
affection for each other was the best part of the show.
(*Copyright © 1994 by Jim Deacy*)

(*Left to right*) Jim Nabors, me, Florence Henderson and Steve Normandale during rehearsals of our lavish production of *The Music Man.*　　(*Copyright © 1994 by Jim Deacy*)

Backstage in Jupiter in 1979, Red Skelton posed for a picture with me.　　(*Copyright © 1994 by Jim Deacy*)

Charles Nelson Reilly, Burt's dear friend, talented actor and master teacher at the Burt Reynolds Institute for Theatre Training, on his yacht *La Bohéme*.

ELAINE—
THANKS FOR TAKING SUCH GOOD CARE OF US!
WE COULDN'T HAVE MADE IT WITHOUT YOU!
LOVE, THE "BRITT" 1990 GRADUATES!

My kids, the Class of 1990 at the Institute. Scot Heminger (*backrow, third from left*) was killed that year.

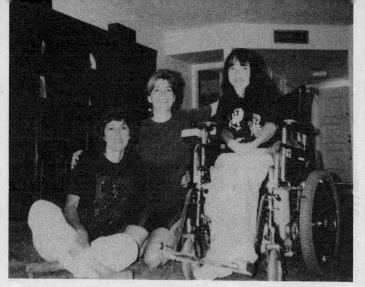

I'm sitting with Melanie Webster (former Institute graduate) and Sally Wagner (President of The Burt Reynold's International Fan Club) in Sally's Florida home.

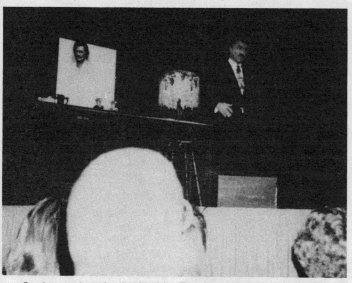

On the road again sharing "An Evening with Burt Reynolds" –twenty-three of them to be exact.

"Barbie and Ken" were alive and well in Jupiter in 1982.
(*Left to right*) Frank Bonner (of *WKRP* fame), Loni, Judy
Murata (Jim Nabors' personal assistant), Jim Nabors
and Burt.   (*Copyright © 1994 by Jim Deacy*)

In 1982, Burt proudly
announced to me, "I'm
filming *Sharky's Machine*
wearing my own hair—or
what's left of it."
(*Copyright © 1994
by Jim Deacy*)

(*Left to right*) James Torrie, estate manager and Tom Ryan, security specialist. We were "The Three Musketeers" ready to rescue Burt day and night—and we usually had to.

Burt and me in 1991 on the set of *Evening Shade*. After he shaved his moustache for the episode, he looked so sweet and vulnerable, I thought he should try to keep it off for a while.

Harry Thomason, TV producer, and superstar Kenny Rogers on the set of *Evening Shade*. To us, they were just two nice guys with gray beards who needed haircuts.

Tammy Wynette, Burt, Whoopi Goldberg and K.T. Oslin on the set of *Evening Shade*.

Burt, Jay Ferguson, one of the stars of *Evening Shade,* and Loni on the CBS/MTM lot. Jay idolized Burt at first, but grew tired of his temper tantrums on set.

Bobbie Ferguson, Jay's mom and manager and one of my best friends, on the studio lot in 1991.

The infamous 1992 accident on the set of *Evening Shade* that sent Burt to the burn center at the Sherman Oaks Hospital.

After Jane Abbott met Burt on the set of *Semi-Tough* in 1976, she became one of his lifelong fans. Her dream of working with Burt came true when she became a regular on *Evening Shade*.

Burt and Loni after the "Royal Wedding" on April 28, 1988.
It turned out as beautiful as I'd planned and everyone
was there...except me.

Singalong with Burt and Loni at home with jazz singer
Carole Hampton and singer/songwriter Bobby Goldsboro.

Quinton was very attached to Janet Spring, his former
nanny, and her husband, John, Burt's house manager until
they were let go.

The happy family in front of their home on Mulholland Drive in Los Angeles.

Miss Ida Turner was Burt's trusted house-keeper in Jupiter for many years until she retired.

Burt and Quinton
are as close
as a father
and son
can be.

Loni and I at a party in 1991. We shared some fun times together.

(*Left to right*) Me, Loni, Sondra Curry (actress friend of Loni and Burt) and Diane McClure (Doug McClure's wife) called ourselves "The Girls Club." Here we are all dressed up for the 1991 People's Choice Awards.

Me, Pam, and my daughter,
Lori Miller in the fall of 1991
at my house for a barbecue.

Pam Seals, the woman who
later became Burt's live-in
girlfriend and me at my
house in 1991. We developed
a very close friendship over
the years.

Loni and Burt—"Barbie and Ken" 1991.

Pam and Burt—"the New Barbie and Ken" 1993.

Norman Golden II, the cute kid who stole the show in *Cop and ½* loved Burt. Burt gave him cowboy boots to match his own and promised to continue their friendship after the filming was over, but didn't. (*Copyright © 1994 Peter Iovino*)

Burt and me on the set of *Cop and ½*.

"Yes, there's life after Burt... but I still miss him."
(*Copyright © 1994 Terry Ganaway*)

pay rent like I'm doing at Jupiter Harbour. It will help you out tax-wise to show it as rental property." Also, my daddy had always taught us never to be beholden to anybody. He'd tell us, if they "lend it to you or give it to you they can always take it back!"

I did remember a former producer who lived in one of Burt's condos for three years and never paid a dime, so when he was fired, he was asked to move immediately with the door almost slamming on his butt on the way out.

"Great!" he responded: "Now get some of the guys from the theatre to help you move your things over there."

A couple of days later I began to move my belongings. During the process of having some of my things brought over, Logan, Burt's father and mother, AND his sister, Nancy, drove up.

Logan came to the door and said, "Hi, Elaine, Burt told us to drive out to look at the new little house he bought, so here we are, but I didn't know you were going to be here. Nancy is with us!"

"Well, I can't run and hide this time. Rita (my assistant) has my car and is on her way over with some of my clothes," I said.

I walked out on the front porch, and Burt's mom and dad were coming up the walkway. I figured Nancy should know I was there before she got inside and had honestly hoped it wouldn't make any difference to her, but I was wrong.

Nancy stopped dead in her tracks and yelled at

Logan, "What's *she* doing here? I'm not coming in as long as she's in there!"

I live here, you self-centered bitch! I wanted to scream, but didn't. After all, this was her brother's house even though I was paying rent, and I didn't want to upset his folks. As they came inside Burt's dad said, "I wish she wouldn't act like that. It's so awful." The three of them walked around the house and even sat down and visited for a moment. . . . Nancy waited outside by the car.

I settled into the house on the beach and it was heaven; however, it was a bit scary after dark. Shortly after I moved in, I learned that Nancy had moved into Burt's condo where I had been living. I don't think she would have done that had she known I had been living there for several months. Her mom later told me that Nancy wanted to move over there, so Bud arranged it for her.

Now the whole scenario was clear to me. That's why he insisted I move into the Bon Air house, but I didn't mind. I was paying the same amount of rent and utilities at Jupiter Harbour, plus now I had the beach. Burt was my boss and my landlord, and all I owed him was an honest day's work and the rent!

When my divorce was final, I paid my ex-husband his half of the equity in our condo in Jupiter Harbour, and I got my own place and my own furniture back and happily moved in.

When I moved out of the Bon Air house, Burt decided to redecorate it. He painted the living-room walls marine blue and the woodwork and

doors off-white. He and I had a great time at one
of the large furniture stores in North Palm Beach,
picking out overstuffed sofas and chairs, tables,
lamps, and all the accessories for the house. He
was fixing it up for Charles Nelson Reilly to use
when he came to teach the apprentices. He had
bought a very ornate white baby grand piano for
the big beach house for Charles's pasta dinner parties and opera nights, so we moved it into the small
den at the Bon Air house. It nearly took up the
entire room, so Burt mirrored the whole wall on
one side to make the room appear larger.

Is It Still My Turn
To Watch Him?

My job description included "baby-sitting" some of Burt's friends when they came to Florida. Three of my most memorable times were with Dom DeLuise, Judd Nelson, and Will Sampson. I was crazy about all of these guys, but they surely kept me jumping!

"Dom's coming down for a week or two, so put him up at Jupiter Harbour," Burt said, calling from California. Burt's condos on the waterway were used to house his friends and the stars performing at the theatre. "We're all so worried about him. He's gotten so fat he can hardly walk. His doctor has put him on a strict diet, so call his wife Carol and find out what he is supposed to eat so you can make sure he sticks to the diet while he's there."

"Okay, Boss," I said, "I'll see that the rehearsal

lunches are geared to it as well. The cast and apprentices won't mind, they're all so conscious of their figures."

When I met Dom at the airport, I was startled to find that he was larger than I had ever seen him in all the years that I've known him. He was limping and walking with a cane, and explained to me his doctor couldn't operate on his hip until he lost some weight. He joked and laughed all the way from the airport, and I couldn't help thinking what a loss it would be should he have a heart attack from all that weight and die. He is truly one of the funniest people I've ever known.

After explaining Dom's situation to the cast and crew at the theatre, they were all willing to give him their support and agreed to eat only those items that were on his diet. When Dom walked into the rehearsal hall, he said, "Hi, everybody," and immediately hurried over to the buffet table. "Oh, great! I see you have my rice cakes!" he exclaimed with less than an ounce of enthusiasm.

When we arrived at his guest condo, the first thing Dom did was to open the refrigerator and food cabinets. We always stocked a guest's condo with all of the food and drinks they liked. Everything was done strictly according to Carol's and the doctor's instructions. He was visibly disappointed by the kitchen's dietetic contents, but quipped, "Oh, well, if I get too hungry, I can eat the furniture. It has no calories!"

Burt was still in California, but he called regularly to check on Dom. He really was worried about his friend's health and wanted to make sure that I was monitoring his diet. The cast and crew continued to support Dom and his diet, although after a few days, some of them would secretly slip out to a fast-food place and really chow down.

One day I came through the entrance gate to my condo and stopped for a minute to chat with the guard on duty. "Boy," he said, "Mr. DeLuise must have had some dinner party last night. He came through the gate and asked if I could help him get his groceries out of the car. We were just changing shifts, so I went over to help him. The front seat, backseat, and trunk were loaded down with bags of groceries."

The next day, while having lunch at Burt's Backstage restaurant, Bruce Nierman, his partner in the restaurant, came over to the table. "When you told me about Dom's diet, I had Dave, our chef, prepare his food very carefully whenever he came in. He was very selective in his choices as if he were programmed. However, Dave said he always drops by after the theatre closes and eats everything left from our dinner hour."

I soon found this to be true with several other restaurants in the area. Everyone loved Dom and he would visit their kitchens singing . . . eating . . . joking . . . eating . . . telling stories . . . eating . . . eating . . . and eating. I finally called Burt and said, "Boss, I give up. He's eating Styrofoam in the daytime and half the town of Jupiter at night!"

Burt said, "If he keeps it up, he's going to have

a heart attack. You've got to talk to him and make him see that!"

"I never could.

"Jesus! What time is it?" my husband Lee asked as the phone screamed into the night.

"It's four A.M.," I said as I grabbed the phone . . . always dreading that something had happened to my kids or my parents. "Elaine, this is Dan Monahan," the frantic voice on the other end of the phone said. Dan was the costar of the *Porky's* films, and was the costar (along with Judd Nelson and Sarah Jessica Parker) in *Wrestlers*, a play that had closed the night before at Burt's theatre.

"Judd's been arrested," he continued, "and is in the Jupiter jail. He had a few too many sakis and while we were at Banana Max (a local hotspot for the younger crowd) he got into a disagreement and things got out of control. Finally the cops were called and they took him to jail."

I immediately got out of bed and started to dress. My husband got dressed to drive over with me. When I arrived, the police explained that Judd was drunk and disorderly and they couldn't settle him down.

"Let me have him and I'll get him on a plane tomorrow," I told them. When Judd came out of the cell, he was yelling and threatening to sue the town of Jupiter, Banana Max, the mayor, and even the mayor's dog! What Judd didn't know was that Mary Hinton, Jupiter's mayor for over ten years and probably one of the most respected politicians in the State of Florida, was not only a good friend of Burt's, but mine as well. He might as well have been threatening a family member.

"Shut up and get into the car," I said. "It's four in the morning and I don't want to hear anything you have to say right now." Lee drove to our condo in Jupiter Harbour next door to where Judd was staying in one of Burt's condos. I drove the car Judd had been using, which the theatre had rented for him.

"Give me my car keys," Judd demanded. "I'm hungry and I'm going to get something to eat."

"No way, this is not your car and you aren't getting into anything else tonight, now go to bed!" I yelled.

"But I'm hungry and there's nothing to eat in here!" he screamed as he stood inside the foyer.

I grabbed the doorknob and yelled, "Call Domino's, they deliver!" Then I slammed the door.

I called Burt the next morning and explained what happened, and told him Judd was planning to stay over for opening night of the new show that night.

"Tell him I'm very disappointed in him and that Jupiter is my town and I want him gone today," Burt said. When I saw Judd the next day, he was like a little boy who was in trouble. I arranged for him to meet with an attorney in my office that afternoon and the limo would take him to the airport directly after. As he passed me on his way out to the car, he stopped at the bottom of the stairs, and looked up at me. "I don't suppose I'll get to come back again, but I'm really sorry and embarrassed about all of this."

"Oh, I'm sure you'll be back. You really gave a fantastic performance and besides, Burt and I both love you and want you back."

"I love you, too, Elaine, and tell Burt and everyone I'm really sorry."

I ran into Judd outside a restaurant in California about five years later and he said to his friend, "Remember I told you about the night I got into trouble in Florida, well this is the lady who bailed me out of jail. God, Elaine, I still feel badly about that."

It reminded me of another similar night, I was awakened from a sound sleep to hear a voice say, "Elaine, this is Randy." It was the night manager from the Sanddollar. "We're trying to close, but I need you to come and get Will," she said. It was almost 3:00 A.M. I knew that she meant Will Sampson, who was re-creating on our stage the role he played as the Native American in *One Flew Over the Cuckoo's Nest*. Will was 6′ 5″ and lean, but very gentle and so proud of his heritage. However, he loved Jose Cuervo Gold Tequila and peppermint schnapps. Sometimes when he had too much to drink, he wouldn't let anyone take him home and would refuse to leave the bar. This was one of those nights.

I walked into the Sanddollar and there he was—

slouched at the bar. "Come on, Will, time to go home," I said very gently.

"Okay, baby, I'm sorry, I just had a few too many." Will knew he was dying of a lung disease, and I think a lot of his drinking was to ease his pain. He could hardly breathe sometimes. He had an oxygen tank in his dressing room and in his bedroom at the condo.

Burt had directed the show and had gone back to California once it opened. He called every day and he always expressed his concern over Will's health.

"When the show closes, see if you can get him to go to the hospital in Miami, the one that took such good care of Mom in 1978," he said one day.

"Boss, you know Will. He has a mind of his own and if he feels he should go, he will," I responded.

"Well, tell him that *I* personally am concerned about him and that I asked you to make an appointment for him to get checked while he's down there. I'm counting on his checking into the hospital. I think he's much sicker than he's letting on. I watched him during rehearsals he has so much trouble breathing it scares me."

I think Will realized that he was getting close to the end, so he did go into the hospital in Miami for a week of rest and Burt kept tabs on him. His onstage performance with Martin Sheen was impeccable, and no one really knew how sick he was.

Will underwent a lung transplant a couple of years later, and was scheduled for a heart transplant as well. He didn't make it, as his heart gave out and he passed away. Burt was saddened by his death and when Will's older son called him to thank him for his kindness to his father, Burt was really touched.

Party Time

Burt really loved entertaining his friends and especially enjoyed planning special events for them. He would fly them into Jupiter from Los Angeles on his private plane and begin the festivities as soon as they arrived. He almost always had them stay at Valhalla, his estate in Hobe Sound, just a few minutes north of Jupiter, so everyone could be together. I would assist him in arranging sleeping quarters, menus, and entertainment for his guests.

Usually the activities included an evening at his theatre, a day at his ranch, and dinner at least once in his Backstage restaurant.

When Charles Nelson Reilly was in town, which was often, he stayed at Burt's lovely oceanfront home on Jupiter Island. Charles always had a huge pasta dinner and opera night or an evening of singing and storytelling with all of Burt's friends and visiting celebrities at the beach house. I usually arranged for a pianist, microphone, and sound system, so it really was a lot of fun for everyone.

Burt was very much at ease in these gatherings. He would always sing, "Roses Suit You So," from the musical *Mack and Mabel* to Loni. It became his and Loni's special song. Loni would send Burt two dozen long-stemmed red roses on special occasions, and always signed the card, "Roses Suit You So, I love you, Loni." During the early eighties, Burt and Loni seemed to be pretty happy most of the time, and on special occasions like these they appeared to be really in love.

On one particular occasion he chartered a beautiful 120-foot yacht to cruise the intracoastal waterway between Jupiter and Ft. Lauderdale. His guests included Ann-Margret and her husband, Roger Smith, Ricardo and Georgianna Montalban, and Robert and Audrey Loggia. He flew everyone in his helicopter to the dock in Ft. Lauderdale for dinner at Burt and Jack Jackson's restaurant.

That night Robert Loggia ordered the largest lobster available, and with Burt egging him on, devoured a record thirteen-pounder. The itinerary included stopping at specialty restaurants along the way and various activities Burt thought everyone might enjoy.

The yacht was beautifully appointed and had a full crew and staff, who waited hand and foot on Burt and his guests. All of the staterooms were also quite nice, and Burt and Loni's master suite was nothing short of exquisite. The first night out, however, my phone at home in Jupiter rang at about 1:00 A.M. "We can't sleep," Burt's voice sounded annoyed. "Our stateroom is next to the engine room and it's so damn noisy it's impossible to get any rest!"

"I'll call the captain and see if he can dock near a nice hotel and I'll have a limo pick you and Loni up," I offered. "When you awaken, the limo can bring you back to the yacht for breakfast and no one will even know you were gone." I called the captain to get his location and when he told me how close he was to Jupiter, I explained the situation and asked him to dock at Johnathan's Landing. I called the limo driver Bob Soli, and arranged for him to pick them up and take them to Valhalla so they could sleep in their own bed. I called the house and alerted the staff.

As I frantically made the rest of the arrangements, the phone rang once again. "I'm sorry we bothered you, honey," said Burt, "but everything is fine now. Since we've docked, the engines are quiet and we're settling in. Thanks a lot, see you tomorrow."

"Say good night, Boss," I muttered as I began dialing Bob's mobile phone—still half-asleep!

B. L. Stryker

"Burt hates for you to leave the theatre, but he wants you to work on his new television series, *B. L. Stryker,* a two-hour series he's starring in. It's going to be filmed in Jupiter, so you don't have to move," David Gershenson said to me early in 1988.

"Great!" I said. "When do we start?"

"Burt will be back in town shortly and will fill you in," he said.

When Burt came back to Jupiter, we met over lunch at his restaurant in his office building next to the theatre. He told me that Lamar Jackson was with the *Stryker* group looking at a nearly empty office building in West Palm Beach as a possible site to locate the production offices. When Lamar joined us, Burt asked how the meeting went. He said they had chosen to take a couple of floors in the building because the rent was cheap. "Oh, by the way, Chief, I told them I wanted the title Associate Producer on the show," Lamar added.

Burt laughed as if he thought Lamar was joking. Lamar was a former Georgia highway patrolman and had always worked as Burt's bodyguard on his films and assisted him in some personal matters, so I don't think Burt thought he was serious.

Lamar looked at Burt very coldly and said, "The *producers* said it was fine!"

Burt looked a little embarrassed as if he had openly offended Lamar and said quietly, "Great, guy, good for you."

Filming each episode on this series was almost like doing a movie each time. It was a two-hour-long episode filmed on location that aired every third week on "ABC's Movie of the Week," alternating with two other episodic movies.

I was out the door before sunup every day ready and waiting for the filming to start. After 9:00 A.M. I usually went into the office to take care of Burt's business relating to *Stryker* as well as any other business he had going and then back on to the set. I must admit that I was a bit like Lucy Ricardo on several occasions and had an uncanny way of accidentally popping into a scene.

On one occasion, I had legal papers for Burt's signature right away, so I went over to the set. They were filming in a tall office building in downtown West Palm Beach that day, and usually when they were rolling, a production assistant was always on the spot to stop anyone from disrupting the shooting. I entered the lobby of the building, said hello to the security guy behind the desk, got on the elevator with some guy who turned out to be an extra, and pushed the button for the sixteenth floor where the set was. As the door to the elevator opened, I stepped directly into a fight scene they were filming. I quickly jumped back into the elevator, but it was too late. The poor extra froze, cowering over in the corner.

"Cut!" the director yelled.

"Who the hell was in that elevator?!" I heard the roar of Burt's voice. I pushed the button to open the door again and stuck my head out.

"It was me, Boss. Sorry, but I guess the 'watchdog' was in the bathroom when I got here," I offered meekly and stepped off as the door closed behind me and the elevator quickly started back down with some poor man whose one shot at a movie career probably ended.

When we were filming a scene involving quite a few cars circling in front of a school, I spotted Tom Bermingham sitting in his Cadillac, a dear friend whom I had not seen in a couple of years. I ran up to the car and jumped in to surprise him. When I did, he quickly moved over. He's a big guy and his arm leaned on the horn, just as the assistant director yelled, "Rolling!"

Tom and I both burst out laughing and I heard Burt's voice somewhere behind me, "That's gotta be Elaine. Where the hell is she?" About that time Tom explained that he was playing hooky from the real estate firm he owned and was an extra in the film that day.

Great! I thought. I *may be taking a lot of days off soon if I don't watch what the heck I'm doing.*

Another early morning we were filming in an office building. I had quite a few papers that his attorneys were anxious for Burt to sign. I waited until the director called, "Cut!" and walked up to Burt with the papers and pen. He and I had discussed the information earlier, so he just needed to sign them. When he finished, I sat down at a desk and began to witness his signature and double-check to make sure I had all the signatures in place.

"Good morning, Elaine!" I recognized the cameraman Nicky Mclean's voice so I didn't look up.

"Good morning, Nicky," I chirped.

"How are you today, Elaine?" he asked.

"Just fine, honey, how're you?" I said as I kept on writing.

"Well," he said sweetly, "I'm just fine, too, . . . and since the script doesn't call for a young lady to be sitting at that desk signing papers, could we ask you to move to another location so we can continue shooting?"

It was 5:30 A.M. and we were all gathered at the ocean in Jupiter just waiting for the sunrise to begin so we could get a shot of Burt standing on a large rock just out in the shallow water, looking out over the ocean with God's hand-painted sky emblazoned in the background.

The crew was all set to shoot and as we stood very close to the water's edge, Burt turned away from us and looked over the horizon. At that moment, everyone except the cameraman turned and started to run up the beach away from the water, all kinds of gear flying in the air, leaving Burt standing on the big rock out in the water. A nurse shark was circling the rock he was standing on, feeding on the little fish around it, and the cameraman didn't miss a frame!

"Thanks a lot, guys!!" Burt yelled up to the crew as the shark moved away and Burt walked back onto shore.

Another time we were filming at Burt's restaurant in Jupiter. The scene involved Burt and one of our former apprentices, Gigi Rice, who is married to Ted McGinley of *Married With Children*, dining, and Burt opens a bottle of champagne. As we were rolling, he did a little schtick that was really funny, and I started to laugh out loud and quickly cupped my hand over my mouth.

"Cut!" said the director and began laughing.

I was so embarrassed, but Burt said, "I knew it was Elaine. That's why I keep her. She thinks I'm funny!"

The Royal Wedding

"Burt and I are getting married, but he won't let me make any of the plans for the wedding." Loni was a bit chagrined.

"Why won't he let you have anything to do with it? I would think he'd rather not have to deal with it," I said.

"He agreed to marry me on the condition that he make all the arrangements. It is to be a small family affair at the chapel on the ranch and that's about it, but I don't think it's fair."

"Then why don't you tell him that. After all, it's your wedding, too," I said.

"Yes, but you know how he is. If I argue with him, he'll call it off."

"Then why do you want to marry him if it's that easy for him to drop it?" I asked.

"Because no one else has been able to marry him, not Dinah, Sally, or anyone else," she said with a smile.

I guess she had forgotten about Judy Carne.

* * *

Burt came into my office one afternoon after their announcement and appeared annoyed. "We're doing a prenuptial agreement so the attorney will be here in a little while. She's not getting anything in Florida."

"Boss, are you sure you want to get married right now?"

"I guess I have to," he replied. "She feels insecure and since we've been living together for the past five years she says it's embarrassing. You *know* how I feel about getting married again."

"Well it's going to be pretty hard to get out of it if you change your mind, so you'd both better be sure."

"I'm sure as hell not going to do it without this prenuptial agreement, so stick around until it's done in case I need you."

During the course of working out the agreement, Loni was very cautious not to upset Burt, who was visibly annoyed at the whole process. When it came time to get the marriage license, Burt asked me to have someone come to the house so it could be done privately. I arranged it and the license was issued.

Burt was having major financial problems at this time, but Loni had been showing me large canary diamonds in the jewelry stores when we went shopping. "This is what I want in my wedding ring," she chirped, "so tell Burt for me, okay?"

When I told Burt that the canary diamonds she had been looking at were between twenty and thirty thousand dollars, he said, "I can't afford that right now! It will just have to be a yellow zirconia until I can afford to replace it with a real diamond."

"Nobody will know the difference, Boss. If I wore it, they'd know, but not on her."

Burt and I designed the ring, and I went to the jeweler and placed the order. When Loni had it appraised for insurance purposes, she found out but carried it off beautifully.

When Burt and Loni then went back to Los Angeles, I began making all the arrangements. I even designed the cake, which was three-tiered and heart-shaped with an Australian lace frosting, topped with marzipan gardenias—Loni's favorite flower. I also made arrangements for the housing and entertainment of all his celebrity friends and even chartered the yacht to take them on their honeymoon cruise.

As I continued planning the wedding, I received a call from one of Burt's staff in California explaining that even though Burt appreciated so much what I was doing to help him get through this, he hoped that I would understand about not being able to go because of his sister. If I was invited, she would refuse to attend.

Loni told me that she felt badly that I couldn't be there and that even though his sister is a very cold person, "blood is thicker than water."

The "small family affair" began to grow as Burt invited all of his celebrity friends and also included many local people. Most of the staff from the theatre, and even the maid from the house, the new houseman and his wife who had only been employed for less than three months were invited. I really began to feel hurt; it was as if everyone in Jupiter was going to the ball but me.

When they returned to Jupiter a few days before the wedding, I went over to his house to bring him up to date on everything. When I began to fill him in, he stopped me and dropped his head and said, "Please don't be hurt, I can't stand for you to be hurt. I love you and my sister so much, but she will walk out of the church and Mom and Pop will be upset and I just can't deal with it. Besides, Loni and I talked about it and we're taking the chopper down to the boat. We want you and Lee to meet us and take the cruise with us. We can have a lot of fun and. . . ."

"Jesus, Boss," I said and I couldn't hold back the tears. "Don't do that to me! I can't go to the wedding, but I can come along for the honeymoon? It's all so humiliating. No thank you. Lee and I are taking our own boat out of town for the weekend."

"Please don't cry, I can't handle this," he said.

I straightened up quickly and said, "It's okay, Boss, just don't bring it up again. I can handle it now," and I began to tell him about all the arrangements I'd made.

As the celebrity guests began to arrive, I got caught up in taking care of their needs. I had gotten to know so many of them over the years. Burt planned a party for his friends at the theatre. We filled all three V.I.P. boxes with the Who's Who of Hollywood and had a wonderful evening, while Loni had dinner next door at Burt's restaurant, Backstage, with her manager, secretary, Burt's sister, and a couple of others. The play at the theatre that night was *I'm Not Rappaport,* starring Ossie Davis, Joe Silver, and Ted McGinley. As everyone was leaving, they hugged me goodbye and said, "I'll see you at the wedding!" One even asked me what I was wearing, and I quipped with a smile, "Oh, I don't want to outshine the bride, so I'm wearing my black-sequined, strapless evening gown!"

Friday afternoon before the wedding, Burt called me to his house in a panic. "I lost the marriage license and Loni's upstairs in hysterics, I need you to get over here now."

I rushed over as the theatre was about ten minutes from his house. When I arrived he was really upset. "I don't know what I did with it, I guess I left it in L.A."

I wanted to ask if he had gotten mad and tore it up, but I didn't. "Well, I have to get on the phone to the clerk of the court's office now and I hope they are still open." It was too late, but I was able to get through to John Dunkle, who had been in that position for many years. I explained the dilemma as Burt paced back and forth saying, "Tell him we have to have another copy today!"

Boss, everyone is gone and the computers are shut down. There is no way to get another one now." John was very apologetic, but there was nothing he could do and Burt was falling apart. Then it dawned on me. "John, back in the old days, the preacher used to fill out the wedding certificate in the family Bible and it was witnessed, will that do?"

"Well, he still has to sign the license for it to be legal."

"Great," I said, "he can do that later, so we'll use the family Bible and the wedding is on!" Burt and Loni were ecstatic.

The day of the wedding, I got a call from Joe Silver. "My wife and I would like to drive to the wedding with you and your husband, if it's convenient."

"Joe, I'm not going to the wedding," I said.

"Why not?" he asked in amazement.

"I have to go out of town today, so I'm going to miss the big event," I told him, trying to sound like everything was fine.

"Wait a minute, Elaine, this doesn't sound right." We had become good friends during the run of the show, and he had teased me about making all the plans for the wedding. "Is it painful for you to go?" he asked.

My God, he thinks I'm in love with Burt and I'm too hurt to go to the wedding, I thought to myself. "No, Joe, it's too painful not to go," and I explained the reason.

"I'm so sorry, it's terrible when family members do that to each other. Well, when you get back, the four of us will go out."

I never really got over the hurt of not being able to attend the wedding, and Burt seemed to forget that I had not gone. From time to time when I was present, Burt used a little flippant remark that he thought was cute in greeting someone: "Hi! Remember me from the wedding?" Everytime he did this, it sent a little pain through me and he'd dart his eyes toward me then quickly look away.

Once he walked into a roomful of people and as I came over to greet him, he said without thinking, "Hi! Remember me from the wedding?"

"Yes, weren't you the one in the white dress?" I quickly shot back. I don't think he ever did that again.

The Golden Child

I received a call the night Quinton was born, August 31, 1988. Burt and Loni were in California and I was attending a performance at Burt's theatre. I was so excited that through adoption he was finally getting the little boy he always wanted that I cried. I remember how special it was when my own children and five grandsons were born, and I just knew this precious little gift would have the love and strength of a father who had been anxiously awaiting his arrival for the past nine months.

When Burt called the next day, his voice kept breaking every time he tried to explain how he felt, and how scared he was the first time he held Quinton because he seemed so fragile. I said, "Well, Boss, you finally have the one thing you've always dreamed of: a little guy to share all those Disney movies you have stacked in the office." I had to laugh when Burt called to tell me that Quinton had rolled over, pulled up in his crib, or whatever he was doing no matter how simple it was at the time.

Having raised my own children and enjoyed my own grandbabies growing up, it was old hat to me, yet I was thrilled that Burt Reynolds was so excited by every move Quinton made.

Burt built offices on the property of Valhalla, so he would be close by when Quinton was awake. Even when we were in the middle of dictation or a serious business discussion, and the nanny would walk down from the house with Quinton, Burt would stop immediately. He'd spend the next hour or so crawling around on his hands and knees with Quinton on his back, or crawling around behind him through his office and mine, riding him back and forth on the library ladder, or rolling around on the floor laughing and playing. I remember Janet, the nanny, laughing and saying, "No one would believe it if you told them the funny things he does with this child."

Burt's desk chair was a big leather wing back, and he would sit Quinton in his lap and read to him. As Quinton got older, he would look at the books and read them aloud to his daddy. I came into the office many times prepared to go over contracts and important matters with Burt, only to have him call me from the house and say, "Go ahead and do what you can, I'm taking Quinton riding on the bike." He would soon sail by on his bicycle with Quinton in his riding seat on the back, helmet and all, squealing with delight.

Many times, I would arrive early and go down to the main house for a cup of coffee and Burt would be sitting at the table with Quinton, who was just a toddler, having breakfast together, just the two of them. Quinton's favorite cereal at that time was Cheerios and he would pick them up one at a time and put one in his mouth, then one in his daddy's mouth until they were all gone. They would both giggle when he dropped one on the floor and Bandit, their cocker spaniel, would quickly lap it up. They had such fun together from the very beginning.

The summer of 1991 Burt did his one-man show, *An Evening with Burt Reynolds,* touring by bus and truck over some twenty-six cities in one-night stands. I was a producer on the tour and every day Burt would say over and over how much he missed Quinton, and that maybe we could have the nanny fly with him to meet us and she could go back and he could travel for a few days with us. I thought it was a great idea because I missed my own grandchildren and I loved Quinton (who called me "Da Yane" because he couldn't pronounce Elaine), so he came on board the bus. Burt sat with Quinton by the window and they would "ooh" and "ahh" at every eighteen-wheeler, cement mixer, bus, train, cow, and horse they saw.

When it was time for him to go home, Burt got very sad and both of them would hold onto each other; Quinton crying, not wanting to leave his daddy, and Burt reassuring him that he would be home soon. I have so many pictures in my mind of the two of them sharing the simple pleasures of their father/son relationship.

Burt always welcomed Quinton on the set of *Eve-*

ning Shade. He would come to rehearsals and sit on his daddy's shoulders when Burt was directing. He knows all the technical terminology his daddy used and at times when people would chatter on the sidelines, Quinton would whisper, "Shhhh, we're rolling." The entire cast and crew all adored Quinton, and he loved coming on the set and having lunch with his daddy in his dressing room. When we had crew picnics and softball games, Burt spent most of the time playing with Quinton. They wandered off together to play, just the two of them, until it was time to go.

Janet and John

"So, what do you think? After all, he used to work for Donald Trump, so this should be a piece of cake for him," I said to Burt after our interview with John Spring for the position as the manager of Burt's estate.

"Let's give him a shot, but please explain that when I come down in the mornings, if I don't say anything, I'm not mad at him. I may have had a bad night and don't want to talk," Burt said.

According to all of the house staff in California and Jupiter, Burt was always very moody in the mornings. Actually he was very quiet during the day and enjoyed reading, listening to music (mostly jazz and the oldies), and watching television.

I hired John who was an Englishman, about five-six, with a very dry wit, and extremely efficient. He took charge of the estate like it was his own home and kept everything in top-notch order. His wife Janet, a registered nurse, lived in their home in West Palm Beach, and John visited her on weekends.

Soon after Quinton was born, Janet was asked to fill in when the full-time nanny had her days off. Janet and John loved Quinton from the very first day. Janet rocked him, sang to him, and she looked forward to caring for him. The full-time nanny stayed only a short time and decided to return to Philadelphia, because the Florida heat and humidity were too much for her, so Burt and Loni asked Janet to take charge of Quinton. Janet was delighted. She had grown so fond of the baby, plus she could move into the apartment with John.

As Quinton grew, John and Janet would take him to the park, or the beach, and even to the grocery store, so he would be exposed to other people in a more natural environment. Unfortunately, when Loni or Burt took him out, the celebrity side would create a stir around him, so they encouraged John and Janet to continue, because when he was with them, no one knew who Quinton was. Neither Burt nor Loni wanted Quinton to be isolated from the world, but wanted to protect him from possible kidnapping or just even becoming a "spoiled little rich kid."

When Burt and Loni moved back to California, John and Janet, their dog and two cats, moved to the West coast as well. If the two of them took a day off, Quinton would ask "Where's my John and Janet?" When they arrived back, he'd squeal, "I knew you'd come back!" He loved them so much.

As Quinton grew, it became obvious that he was a very bright child and had developed a bit of an English accent. "Daddy, can we take a bubble *bahth* together?" he'd ask Burt. "Yes, Quinton, we'll take a bubble *baahhth* together," he'd say. He began to walk just like John and acquired many of the same mannerisms. When John and Janet talked about Quinton, you would have thought he was their own. I have to say, although they had accepted these surroundings as their home, neither of them ever tried to be a part of the family. They always referred to Burt and Loni as "Mr." and "Mrs." even though that precious little boy was creeping into their very souls.

There were times when Janet would become a little impatient with Loni, because if Quinton was made to sit in a chair for disciplinary reasons, Loni would come into the room and pick him up and hold him and ask, "What did you do to make Janet mad at you?" Janet explained to Loni on many occasions that it was very difficult for a child to determine that he had done something unacceptable, if she kept doting on him every time he was reprimanded. Burt offered no discipline, and Quinton was beginning to test his perimeters with each of them, as any child of three or four will do.

John called me on several occasions at my office on the CBS/MTM lot and spoke of his and Janet's frustrations. He told me that he had spoken to Burt about the problems they were encountering, but he said Burt would just get too upset and either start screaming at Loni or just refuse to talk about it. His standard line was, "I can't deal with that now! I've got enough of my own problems on the set! You guys will just have to work it out with her!"

As Burt and Loni began having greater difficulty in their marriage, Burt stayed away from home more and more. He stayed in the editing room of *Evening Shade* for hours or he'd rehang all the pictures in his dressing room and production offices until the wee hours, then he'd go home, get a couple of hours' sleep, and awaken early to go back to work. According to Janet and John, Loni was constantly on the go, shopping, having lunch or dinner with her friends, and really didn't spend a lot of time with Quinton.

Quinton became more and more unruly and belligerent. As in most cases of marital disputes, children don't necessarily have to be present when their parents are fighting to know that there is a problem. They sense it when they're around them, and they begin to feel very insecure. Even at his young age, Quinton was cognizant of the friction in his once happy home, and in time he became more and more attached to Janet and John.

Loni, however, had no control over him whatsoever, and many times would have to cut her shopping trip short, because "Quinton was so unruly it was embarrassing." Burt was away from the house so much, he couldn't bring himself to discipline Quinton, so the responsibility of setting boundaries became Janet and John's.

Since Loni couldn't handle Quinton alone, the Springs didn't have a day off for four months, because there was no one to take care of Quinton.

Eventually Jean Jensen, Loni's secretary and friend, did cover an occasional weekend, but de-

veloped slight heart problems and was unable to
continue.

Janet had voiced her concern to me over the last
year I was with Burt that she had on many occasions
attempted to sit down with Loni and involve her
with raising Quinton. But Loni slept until very late
in the mornings, then spent hours getting ready to
go shopping, and there was no time for him. This
was expressed to Janet by a former nanny, as well,
who was concerned that the "little boy was not as
involved with his mother as much as he should be."

Janet told me that when she would inquire of
Loni what she wished to be done for Quinton or
any suggestions she might have for the day-to-day
raising of the child, Loni would tell her that she
wouldn't change a thing; she and Burt were happy
with things the way they were.

One day Janet and John met me for lunch. I
was telling them that Loni had been questioning
me about Burt's girlfriend and that she had said
Burt's sister and her manager tried to convince her
it was me. They both said she questioned them
about whether there was anything romantic going
on between Burt and me. They reassured her it
was not true.

I've been asked by some people since the divorce
as to why I didn't tell Loni about Pam, because
Loni and I had been friends as well before. I let
Loni know from the very beginning of her relationship with Burt that my first loyalty would al-

ways be to Burt. He was my boss and I needed my job, and if she wanted to know anything, she'd have to ask him, not me. There were a lot of things over the years that I could have told Burt about Loni also, but I chose not to get involved in their domestic problems.

John and Janet were finally getting a much needed vacation. Burt told them just before they left that he loved them and wanted them with him "until the day he died." A week after their return, Burt was at the studio, Janet was upstairs bathing Quinton, and John and Loni were in the kitchen when the phone rang. Loni answered it and said, "John, it's Lamar for you," and left the kitchen. Lamar told John that Burt wanted them to take a few days off and go to a motel to stay. They were told to leave the house that night before Burt got home, because he couldn't take the tension anymore and Loni was really making things tough for him.

John said that he called Lamar the next day and was told to come to the house on Saturday and meet with him and Burt to settle things. When John arrived for the meeting, Burt, according to Lamar, had gone away with Loni and Quinton for the weekend and the Springs were to pack their things and move back to Florida as soon as possible.

I was in Florida visiting my parents at the time and when I picked up my messages from my phone in California I heard John's voice, "Elaine, Janet and I are at a motel. We've been fired and have to move back to Florida right away. Please give us a call when you get this message."

John had told me previously Loni wanted everyone gone who was close to Burt and had overheard her on many occasions demanding that he get rid of Lamar, John, Janet, me, and even Bandit. Apparently, she had succeeded.

I immediately called them when I returned and they both were very upset. "What about little Quint? What will he think? What will they tell him about where we are? When we came back from our vacation, he ran and hugged us both, I knew you'd come back! I knew you'd come back!"

"I'll be back in L.A. day after tomorrow and we'll get together," I told them.

It was very sad, listening to them as they poured their hearts out over their concern for Quinton and also now facing the issue of where to get another job. We still keep in touch. Janet went back to nursing and, after eighteen months, John found a part-time job. When you're past fifty, it is very difficult to find employment even though you have many good years left. Janet recently told me that she and John had felt like "empty canisters" for over a year, but were now getting their life put back together. Even though they still miss Quinton terribly, she says they at least had each other for support through all of the trauma.

Pam

"I talked to Vic last night and a couple of girls he knows from Tampa are coming to the theatre tomorrow, so make it special for them, okay?" Burt was calling me from California.

Burt asked me on many occasions to give special attention to friends of his and to comp their visit. Vic Prinzi was Burt's *real* college roommate at Florida State University, not like so many others claiming to be. I always felt that if there was a reunion of all the folks who claimed to have gone to school with Buddy Reynolds they would fill the Coliseum in Rome, and half of them would be about ten years younger than Burt. Nevertheless, I always made sure any of Burt's visiting friends received V.I.P. treatment.

Pam Seals, an attractive blonde, and her friend Beth attended a matinee, and I introduced myself to them at the bar in the cocktail lounge at the theatre. I remember thinking how pretty Pam was and with her drop-dead figure, she created quite a stir with the male staff members and patrons in the theatre lobby. She had a winsome smile and an incredible sense of humor. I liked her immediately.

Burt called me later that evening and asked, "Did the girls have a good time?"

"Yes, Boss, and they really enjoyed the show," I responded.

When he asked me about the girls, I could tell from his voice that he was interested in Pam especially. Many times in the past he had me or someone working for him introduce him to a particular girl he had noticed at a party, in a group, in a restaurant, or anywhere we might be. He really was something to watch when he was "smitten" by an attractive woman. His whole "macho" demeanor changes. He drops his head a little, lowers his brown eyes, and smiles sweetly as he begins his flirtation. His target is immediately disarmed by his charm and the courtship begins.

I can't remember ever seeing Pam again until we began shooting *B.L. Stryker* in 1988, and she came to the set with one of Burt's single friends. She appeared to be dating this guy and Burt gave her a scene in the episode we were shooting. I talked with her quite a bit and she was very sweet and was very nervous about doing the shot. Pam, being from a small town outside of Tampa, Florida, and I from a smaller town outside of Wilmington, North Carolina, shared a lot in common. I saw her a few times after *B. L. Stryker,* but she was always with a male friend of Burt's.

When Burt became interested in seeing Pam, he

did not want me to know about it. He knew that Loni and I did a lot of things together, so he always made arrangements to see her through Lamar Jackson, who was his former bodyguard and usually accompanied him when he was filming. Lamar told me about "the Face" as Burt affectionately called her, yet I never let on to Burt that I knew who she was. It really was none of my business and didn't affect my responsibilities at the time. Lamar made all her flight and hotel arrangements in his name.

One day I was working in my office located just down the driveway from the main house at Valhalla. I needed an address from the Rolodex at the house, so I buzzed John Spring, who managed the estate at that time. He was out at the moment, so I walked up the driveway, through the garage, and into the hallway toward the first door on the left, which was John's office. As I entered the hallway and walked toward the office, a pretty blonde crossed the hall at the other end that entered the kitchen. She had a frightened expression on her face and looked away immediately.

I went directly into the office for the Rolodex and got the needed information. When I walked back down to my office, I buzzed Burt who was upstairs in his bedroom at the house.

"Sorry, Boss, I guess I frightened the heck out of your friend. Please understand that I have known about her for some time now, but had no reason to tell you. I am not judgmental as you know, so there is no reason for either of you to be uncomfortable. Your personal life is your business."

"Well, she was a little embarrassed, and I told her that you have been with me for so many years, you'd understand.

"She really is a sweet girl and has a great sense of humor, so if you get to know her, you'll be crazy about her."

I had known for some time that Burt and Loni were having problems in their marriage, so it didn't come as a surprise to me that either of them might look for someone to fill the void.

"She really likes you a lot," Burt said over the phone. "I hope you'll become friends."

We did become friends. Pam is one of the funniest people I have ever known and would help anyone out who needed it. Her mother, Edie, is a very quiet, sweet lady who looks much younger than her years. Pam and Edie lived together in Lutz, outside of Tampa, Florida, and got along so well together. They obviously love each other very much.

Pam works out every day in a gym and has a magnificent body. She has made me so aware of healthy, nonfatty foods that I can't even enjoy a package of peanuts on an airplane without checking to see how many fat grams are inside. She does, however, drive to McDonald's every morning for a diet Coke with lots of ice, and often will order pancakes with well-done bacon to go. She really loves Burt and tries to take care of him. She has hundreds of beautiful outfits he has bought her over the years, beautiful jewelry, paintings and pictures. Burt had me use family or friends' names instead of hers to identify the gift purchases for the accounting firm, which proved to be a little awkward for me in later years.

I maintained "good" relationships with both of the women in Burt's life. While I worked for him, he needed me to be friends with them, but remain discreet. I shopped for gifts from Burt for Loni as well as Pam for birthdays, Christmas, and special occasions.

He Can't Hurt Me,
He's My Brother

Coach Jim Nicholson, a high-school football coach, who was Burt's best friend growing up, was legally adopted by Burt's parents in the late seventies. After the adoption, he, his former wife Jo, and their son and daughter, Jamie Jo and Buddy, acquired the Reynolds name and dropped the "Nicholson" forever.

I met Jim at the Reynolds ranch. He was a very warm man who loved his children very much. Burt's family had special tables reserved for opening nights at the theatre as long as he owned it, and Jim was always there with his wife and children, so I saw him rather frequently.

Jim, as Burt tells it, just went home with him one day during high school and Burt announced to his parents, "This is my new brother and he's going to live with us." Burt's father was the chief of police in Rivera Beach, and he and Burt's mom were fond of Jim Nicholson, who they knew was from a broken home plagued by alcoholism, so they allowed him to move in. Burt and Jim were inseparable in high school and went to Florida State University together to play "big-time college football," their first love.

However, Burt suffered major injuries to his knees in a near-fatal car accident while heading home at high speed from college for the holidays. Ending his hopes for a professional football career, he moved back home to Rivera Beach. One day he went over to Palm Beach Junior College and signed up for an English literature course taught by Dr. Watson B. Duncan III, who became his mentor. Dr. Duncan directed him in his first play, *Outward Bound* that won Burt a Florida Drama Critics Award and a scholarship to Hyde Park Playhouse in New York. . . . The rest is history.

As Burt's career began to soar and Jim's first marriage began to fail, Burt invited his "brother" to move into his home in California. Jim gave up his coaching job, moved in with Burt, and after joining the teamsters union, began a new career in the movie business.

Unfortunately, some of the people around Burt became jealous of Jim's closeness with Burt and started creating ripples in the tide of calm waters. After a period of time, Burt began to listen to the "sharks," and his brother found himself standing on the outside looking in. Jim, to this day, says that he does not understand what happened and that Burt just refused to talk to him about it and completely cut him off.

After about five years, Burt allowed his brother to reenter his life. Knowing his brother's volatile personality, Jim never broached the subject as to why Burt closed the door on him.

In 1990 we were in Florida and Burt was producing and directing Tammy Wynette's new music video at his ranch; Jim was on the set and a young girl we had all gotten to know, who was dying of cancer, arrived to watch the taping.

Burt was not happy with the way things were going at that moment and was reshooting a particular scene when she arrived. Jim had not heard the "rolling" call and began to greet the girl. Burt called "Cut!" and ran over and popped Jim on the back of the head so hard it almost knocked him over. Jim turned blood-red and looked at his brother with such a hurt expression it broke my heart. Burt tried to shrug it off with a forced laugh. "I should have known it was my own brother," he wryly observed and continued with the taping.

I went over to Jim and asked if he was all right. The people around him were very angry at Burt for hitting Jim. Jim looked at me, his face still red and tears in his eyes, and said, "If that had been anybody else, I'd have decked him, but he's my brother, so it didn't hurt as bad."

After the scene was over, Burt started walking toward me crossing a bridge over a small brook. I stopped him and said, "I know you didn't mean to hit him that hard, but you almost knocked his head off!"

He dropped his head and said, "I can't believe I hit my brother like that in front of everybody. I know he's hurt, but I can't deal with this now."

"Yes, you can. He's coming across this bridge right now, so turn around and meet him and hug him so he and everybody else here will know you're sorry," I said.

And, Burt did just that. I always will believe that he really wanted to and just needed a nudge.

Catalogs and Gift Buying

"Honey, they've got some great diamond watches for men and women on QVC right now, so turn on your television set. I need you to order some for me. These will be great for the apprentices at Christmas and you can have them engraved. Maybe you'd better order six extra of each, so we will have them for special occasions," Burt's called to tell me.

"God, doesn't he ever sleep?" I thought. It was 1:00 A.M.

"Okay, Boss, I have it on, but I need your credit card number," I said, grabbing my ever present notepad from the bedside table. I was as familiar with these calls as I was with him handing me a stack of catalogs with everything from clothing, videotapes, jewelry, toys, music cassettes and CDs, electronic equipment, and anything else you could buy from direct mail. At one point when he was in grave financial trouble, I used to hide the catalogs from him, but they came so frequently to the office and to his homes, it was impossible to keep him from ordering. He would mark pages and pages of items, if he liked a particular sweater or shirt, he would order one in every color.

He really was very generous and ordered gifts for anybody, for no special occasion. He loved giving gifts, but always had trouble receiving them. Many times friends sent him very expensive and unique gifts. If they came past my desk, I made sure he sent a thank-you, but unfortunately, if they went to his house many times they were not acknowledged.

I remember a few years ago David Gershenson gave him a massage table that cost a couple of grand. Burt didn't acknowledge it and David was hurt, despite the fact that he had told me in the past, "Burt never says thank you so don't expect it."

I found it difficult to buy gifts for him, because he had so much, and I really couldn't afford to buy anything unique. One Christmas I found a book of handwritten autobiographies of movie stars in the twenties and thirties in a used-book store. Each biography was one or two pages only, but written by the stars themselves. The cover had water damage and the price of the book was $2. I tried to locate the publishing company to possibly order a new one, but the book had been out of print for so many years and the publishing company had long since closed. I decided to send it to him anyway, thinking he'll enjoy it and it's the thought that counts. I was right. Burt called me from California just to tell me that he was reading it at the moment and how much he was enjoying it. I told him that somebody's cat must have peed on the cover, but it was out of print and I couldn't get a new one. He said, "I don't care about the cat pee, the book is great!"

Burt almost always personally selected gifts for his family and friends. Even though he had his longtime friend Patty Fuller purchase several items from a Christmas list for him, he always chose the gift himself. Many times he had me pick up gifts for him and he hated it when his business manager complained about the cost. Many items were purchased for women who were strictly friends, but he had me place them under family names when they were reported to the business manager so Loni would not be jealous. When Burt began his relationship with Pam, I hid the gifts under the names of his sister-in-law, his niece, the girls who worked at the ranch, or whoever—in case a question should arise because there were so many purchases.

When Burt and Loni married, she said that I should continue to be responsible for gifts for the employees at the ranch, Burt Reynolds Productions, apprentices, friends (that Patty Fuller was not taking care of) and his family members with the exception of his mother, father, and sister, Nancy.

One time Burt called me from L.A. around 7:30 P.M. on Sunday. "Hi, it's me. Mom's birthday is today, and I can't believe I forgot about it. Did you take care of it?"

"No, Loni's been taking care of your mom, dad, and sister for the last few years, so I didn't give it a thought," I responded.

"Oh God, you have to get something to her for me. I don't want her to know I forgot," he said frantically.

"Boss, it's after seven-thirty here and on Sunday, so there is not a store open that would have anything suitable," I explained, plus my husband and I were to meet my friend Barbara Voight at her club for dinner at 8:00 P.M.

"You've got to help me out, I can't stand her not getting something from me," he cried. "This could be her last birthday!"

"How about if I go to the jewelry store first thing tomorrow morning and get something for her. I'll call and tell her it didn't arrive on time," I offered.

"No," he started to panic, "It's not the same as on her birthday, please try to come up with something."

"Okay, give me a minute to think," I responded as I opened my jewelry drawer to select earrings for dinner. "Wait, I just found the beautiful gold choker with the teardrop zirconia pendant you gave me for Christmas. It's still in the velvet box and I haven't worn it yet."

"It's perfect, and I'll get you another one. Can you take it over to her tonight?" he asked.

"Okay, consider it done, Boss," I replied. I sent my husband over to the club to meet my friend, quickly wrapped the box, wrote a note saying what I knew Burt would say to his mom, and drove out to the ranch, sang "Happy Birthday" from Bud and went to dinner. This was one of many incidents that I filled special-occasion emergencies with gifts Burt had given me. Incidentally, he usually forgot to replace them.

California, Here I Come!!

"I need to talk with you about something, but I have to go upstairs first and get some sleep. Please come back in about two hours and I'll be awake then," Burt said to me. He had just landed on the dock in front of his house, and Logan was taking his chopper back to the ranch. My mind was racing, trying to figure out what was happening. It was early in 1990, *B. L. Stryker* had been cancelled, and he was returning from California. I knew he had been meeting with Linda Bloodworth Thomason and her husband Harry, hoping to get a new television series with them. I couldn't read the look on his face, because there appeared to be some concern. I hoped he was able to work out a deal, because he really was counting on the regular money coming in.

When I came back to the house, he was alert and waiting for me. He didn't look up as he started to speak. I had already figured that when *Stryker* ended I would stay on as his executive assistant, handling correspondence, social functions in Florida, and whatever else he needed since I had still been doing that for years. I was also actively involved on the Board of The Burt Reynolds Institute for Theatre Training, so I knew there was plenty I could do to justify a basic salary.

"Now just hear me out," Burt began. "I got the series called *Evening Shade* and I'm really nervous about a half-hour weekly show filmed in a studio. Doing *Stryker* was more like a movie. It was two-hours long and filmed on location. I know your family is here, but I need you to go to California for just two or three months to help me get set up. We'll get you an apartment close to the studio. It won't cost you anything, and you can come home to Florida every weekend. Please talk to Lee about it and let me know right away."

I had such mixed emotions. I was excited about working on a sitcom, but I also had remarried three years earlier and legally adopted my husband's daughter, who was fifteen at the time. Her mother had died of cancer when she was eleven and she had been living with her dad for two years after his last divorce. She was now eighteen and had become my "baby girl" and we were very close. But both of them encouraged me to go to California.

"Elaine," Harry Thomason said near the end of the first season of *Evening Shade*, "if you can get someone to handle some of your responsibilities for Burt, we'd like to move you up to associate producer on the show. You've really taken an interest in the show and we think you'd be an asset to us. Taking care of Burt consumes so much of your time and you need to be free of some of the day-to-day stuff in order to take the position."

Wow! I had been spending a lot of time in the editing room with Burt and Harry simply because I loved the postproduction side of the business, but I was surprised that I was being given this opportunity so soon. However, before I accepted this wonderful offer, my position as Burt's personal assistant had to be filled. I began to wrack my brain to try to think of someone who could take care of him, someone who already knew his habits and personality so they could slide in fairly easily.

A few weeks prior, Scott Jackson, who had been a cocktail waiter and bartender for ten years at Burt's theatre, had called. "Elaine, you always told me I should move to Los Angeles and now I think I'm ready to do it. If you know of any jobs, schlepping or whatever, please let me know." Scott was really a good employee and on several occasions I tried to move him into a management position at the theatre. He wanted no part of it. He told me that the hours were too long, the responsibility too great, and the pay would be less than he could make waiting tables. Scott was personable and efficient, and the theatre patrons loved him. He is also one of the funniest guys I've ever known. Whenever I was planning a dinner party for Burt or any kind of special function, I could always count on Scott to help keep things in order.

We were planning the one-man road show during our summer hiatus from *Evening Shade* at the time Harry made the offer to me, so a light went on. Scott could answer the phones for Burt Reynolds Productions while we were on the road, and Burt could see that he was capable of more than just passing around drinks, plus he could gradually get used to functioning in an office atmosphere. He really did a great job. When we came back, I was officially promoted to associate producer and Scott became Burt's assistant and handled a lot of my former duties.

God, I loved being in the editing room. I was told when I assumed my new position by the former associate producer that the on-line session only required my presence to check the credits for the show and make sure the names were spelled correctly, proper titles were given, etc. I soon discovered as I sat for hours in those sessions with the editor that it was much more involved than that. It was amazing to see the smallest details that can get overlooked, such as stock shots of the outside of homes, stores, parks, etc. One shot could show a house in dead winter and later in the show a house in the same neighborhood with green grass and spring flowers. These errors can be corrected at this point, but, as Harry Thomason once said to me during my first season in a mixing session when I brought something to his attention, "I'll tell you just like I tell Linda, it's too late to fix it when it gets here, so part of your job will be to watch for it before it leaves the editing room." It was a point well taken.

Once we were filming a large wedding which was already going into the late, late hours and well into "gold," the term used to indicate well over budget and double dollars, which always called the budget guys and studio heads onto the scene. I noticed that Burt and all the men in the wedding party, ushers included, were wearing their boutonnieres on the wrong side of their jackets.

"Wait!" I yelled just as they were starting the wedding march.

"What the hell is the matter?" Burt said.

Everyone was tired and definitely stressed out at this point. I realized that I had stuck my neck out again, so I said, "All of the boutonnieres are on the right side of the jackets instead of the left. I know the men watching won't notice, but millions of women will think we don't know any better!" I felt a bit foolish at that point, but they stopped and switched them over.

Burt Wins Again

I attended the People's Choice Awards in 1991. Burt received an award for Favorite Male Performer In A New Television Series for *Evening Shade*. It was his eighth People's Choice Award. This award is a beautiful crystal flame with applauding hands etched inside. When Burt asked me to have someone at the ranch ship the other seven to L.A. so he could display them in his office, I called Lenore Haas, who has worked at the ranch for years, to have them shipped to us. She assigned the task to Bubba, one of the ranch hands. When the box arrived at the office, all but one was broken into several pieces.

I quickly contacted the people associated with the awards and was told that each one was hand-blown and only done once a year for the award ceremony. They cost approximately $2,000 each to make, so there were no extra ones sitting around to buy and inscribe. We applied for the insurance, but it didn't replace the awards. Burt said with a laugh, "Maybe we could glue the pieces together into some abstract crystal art object. When anyone asks what it is, I can tell them it's eight years of what the public thinks of me."

I was thrilled at Burt's nomination for an Emmy for *Evening Shade*. I really felt he was going to win and since I was an associate producer on the show, it was even more meaningful. Burt's girlfriend, Pam, was in town as well as his longtime friend, Vic Prinzi who also lived in Florida. Pam told me that she and Vic were going to watch the Emmy broadcast together and have dinner, so I selected a dress and had a manicure, planning to attend the awards. A couple of hours before it was time to leave, the phone rang. It was Burt. "Honey, I know you were looking forward to going tonight, but I'm really feeling guilty about 'the Face' (his affectionate name for Pam). Would you stay with her and you girls have a fun night out together instead? I'm so nervous about tonight and I really need you to do this for me."

"Damn, Boss," I said, "It's my show, too, and we have several nominations. I've really looked forward to going, and Pam understands that. She and Vic are going to be together. . . . I even had my nails done!"

"I'm sorry, I don't want to hurt you, but I can't stand the thought of her just sitting there with Vic."

"Okay, but I have a feeling you're going to win tonight and I really wanted to be there." But he was the boss, and a long time ago so I couldn't tell him to drop dead and go anyway, so I just quietly said, "I'm okay, just go get your Emmy and we'll be watching."

"Sam," and Alan Levi lived down the street from me and had a full-size screening room in their house. They had invited me to watch the Emmys with them and a few of our mutual friends if I didn't attend the ceremony. Pam was really upset that I was not going to the awards with Burt, and knew when I told her I decided not to go that Burt had asked me to stay with her. She'd have no part of it and insisted on being with Vic instead, so I attended the party at the Levis'. When I spoke with Burt later that night, he was choked up with emotion. "I never thought I'd win tonight."

"Well, I did."

Loni and Me

Loni and I had some good times together right up until just before her breakup with Burt. When she came to Florida, she really didn't have any special girlfriends to do things with, so occasionally we went shopping, out to lunch, or just hung out together.

One afternoon I got a call from her. "Hi, it's Loni, Burt and I were invited to go to New York for the grand opening of the Planet Hollywood. He can't go, but I thought you might like to go with me. Ann-Margret is doing her show, so we can do both."

"Great! I'd love to," I said. "You know I'm crazy about her." I had gotten to know Ann-Margret and her husband, Roger Smith, because they were longtime friends of Burt's and came to Florida quite often. She is absolutely a beautiful woman and is very shy, but has a great sense of humor and adores her husband and their cats (who, incidentally, live in small "kitty condos" on their back porch).

We flew up on the MGM-Grand jet, a beautiful flight catering to the rich and famous. Loni and I were in a small compartment a bit like the private compartment on a train. Our seats were side by side in very comfortable armchairs that were on short tracks to allow you to pull your seat forward and tilt it all the way back for sleeping, if necessary. During the flight to New York from Los Angeles, we enjoyed the services offered by the airline and just chatted about everything currently happening.

As the plane began its approach into the airport in New York and started to descend, evidently my seat had not been locked into place and in the middle of a sentence, I just slid past Loni to the end of the track. It was like some comedy sketch in a movie. I envisioned myself passing all the passengers and stopping in the cockpit saying, "Are we almost there yet?"

Planet Hollywood was wall to wall people, and Ann-Margret's show was spectacular. We had a great time.

We had "girls' night" at Sondra Currie's house on many occasions. Sam, as we called her, is married to Alan Levi, a producer, and they have a beautiful house in Sherman Oaks, California. Sam, Loni, me and a few other women friends, would get together and have dinner, champagne, and girl talk.

Once, just before Valentine's Day, we decided to surprise our husbands or boyfriends so we all brought over our sexiest lingerie and took Polaroid pictures of each other in seductive poses. It was all very innocent and fun. The whole group of us was basically modest and the pictures were very conservative; stretching out on the top of the grand piano holding a glass of champagne while trying to look sensual and not burst out laughing, or lying on the floor in a silk nightie with an arm wistfully over the head—nothing for the porn magazines, that's for sure. We even took group pictures, smiling like a bunch of teenagers at a slumber party. At the end of the evening, the pictures were lined up on the dining-room table, about fifty of them, and each of us selected the "keepers" and then set about cutting up all of the others into tiny, minute pieces. Those pieces were mixed together and put into many trash containers so they never fell into the wrong hands. It was as if we feared some "puzzle maniac" was lurking about ready to put all the pieces together again.

A couple of years ago, our group planned a surprise birthday party for Loni at Sam's house. She was really surprised and we were all having a great time . . . until she said to me, in front of the group, "Elaine, everyone thinks Burt is having an affair because he hasn't made love to me in over a year—do you think he is?"

She knew better than to ask me that. "Loni," I answered, "I don't think Burt has time for an affair. He never stops working long enough."

"Yes, but a couple of people told me they feel he's having an affair with you, because you're closer to him than anyone and have been with him longer."

I certainly hadn't counted on that one. The blood drained from my face and I felt sickened by the accusation. "Loni, look at me. I'm a fifty-two-year-old grandmother of five with no face-lifts. Do I look like someone your husband would have an affair with?" I was so hurt, I wanted to cry. "I am more like a mother to him and it would seem rather incestuous," I said to her. "I can take a polygraph test right now and attest to the fact that I've never even seen him without his hair or in his underwear, much less naked!

In all the years at his theatre, I got used to actors walking around in various stages of undress backstage, but I always knocked before entering a dressing room. Burt was no different. Even when we traveled on the bus during the road show, I slept on the sofa in front in my sweat suit, Lamar slept in the bunk area in the center of the bus, and Burt had his own bedroom in back"

"I don't really believe it's you," Loni continued, "but a couple of people have said it, so I felt I had to mention it."

"Who would dare say a thing like that?!!" several of the girls cried at the same time. They all instantly came to my defense.

"Every time a woman is successful in her job, somebody thinks it's because she's sleeping with the boss," one of them yelled. The other girls were just as angry at the accusation. "Tell us who it was and we'll straighten them out!" another offered.

Loni said, "That isn't necessary now because I don't believe it anyway."

Later, in trying to lend some credibility to her reason for bringing it up at the party, she disclosed the names of the people who insisted that I was his girlfriend. One of them was Linda Jensen, her manager, who was at her birthday party, and the other was his sister, Nancy.

A couple of years after Loni and Burt were married, she made a remark to me that I performed almost all the tasks a wife did: hostess, confidante, taking him to the doctor, suggesting stories for him to tell at the dinner table, going with him to a bookstore or record shop. . . . Hell, no wonder she figured I slept with him, too! Strangely enough—and Burt will bear this out—I don't think it ever even entered our minds. There was never that kind of chemistry between us.

At this point in my life and at this writing, if I had ever been romantically or sexually involved with Burt, I'd say so, but it didn't happen.

Travels with Burt

"I'm getting my act together and taking it on the road," Burt said tongue in cheek "I would like to do it this summer," he said to Ken Kragen, his new personal manager who replaced David Gershenson, who was summoned to assist in putting the project together. Ken manages some of the top talent in the business today including Kenny Rogers, Trisha Yearwood, and Travis Tritt. He is one of the nicest men I've ever met and a dedicated family man.

"We'll call it, *An Evening With Burt Reynolds,* and Burt will tell all those great stories he's been telling over the years," Ken said.

"I'll call around tomorrow and get some feedback on possible venues." Ken was enthusiastic and ready to get things going. The set was designed as a den in Burt's house, with a sofa and cocktail table, a small bar, plants, and a rear projection screen for slides and film clips above a very large credenza. John Dayton, who offered his technical expertise and guidance, really helped put the show together. We gathered pictures of family, friends, and a huge collection from his career, and had them made into slides and put them together with a few film clips and transferred them to laser disc. David Dansky, Joe Bianchi, Dennis Brook, and Michael Gladstone, some of the best technicians I've ever worked with, made up our crew.

We flew to North Carolina to put the show together at the Flatrock Playhouse, in Flatrock . . . just a stone's throw from Asheville. With enough slides, film clips, and stories to last a lifetime, we went into the theatre, set up, and began our first "tech" rehearsal at 9:00 in the morning. We worked continually and only stopped to go to the bathroom. Our food and drinks were brought in so we never saw the outside again for twenty-four hours. By the next morning, we knew we had a winner.

We had a lot of "misadventures" during the "road show." One night in Sarasota, Florida, Burt stopped the performance and called to me from the stage.

"What's going on back there, Elaine?"

"Sorry, Boss, the computer has a glitch," I whispered loudly, as the slides accompanying his anecdotes began flipping around in the computer as well as on the screen center stage. "We'll have it fixed in a minute."

"Well, what the hell am I supposed to do out here while you fix it?" he asked.

"Just tell the stories without the slides and we'll catch up," I told him.

The engineer operating the computer was in a panic. The laser discs arrived from Los Angeles with the changes late in the day, and we had to load them in at the last minute without a run-through. A list of the anecdotes that coincided with the slides and film clips were always placed on top of the bar on the set so he could refer to them if needed.

"Elaine," he said from the stage again, "my glasses aren't on the bar, so I can't read the lineup!"

"Oh Christ!" the stage manager said. "I forgot to put them out."

"Where are they?" I asked.

"Behind the bar on the shelf."

By that time the entire crew was in a panic. I didn't know what else to do, so I walked out on stage, reached behind the bar, and bringing out Burt's glasses, I said, "Hi, Boss, looking for these? Can I fix you a drink while I'm here?"

"Yes," he said, "a triple vodka tonic! What happened?"

"Well," I began, "the disc got here late today from L.A."

He turned to the audience of about fifteen hundred people and repeated, "The disk got here late today from L.A."

I continued, ". . . and the computer got confused."

He repeated to the audience, "And the computer got confused."

"So here is the story you should tell now," I said as I pointed to the notes on the bar, "and we'll catch up with you on the computer, okay?"

He grinned and started the next story. We finally caught up with him, finished the show, and he received a standing ovation. Everyone thought the glitch was part of the show.

One of Burt's favorite stories when he did his road show was about a horse that he rode in the film *Navajo Joe*. The low-budget film was made in 1967 in Italy.

When they brought over the horse Burt was to use during the film, he was a pathetically ragged and lean animal with a straggly mane and tail. When Burt saw him he told the director, "This horse is supposed to be a paint . . . with big white spots on him. I'm playing the part of an Indian and I'm supposed to ride a paint horse!"

Finally after much discussion, the same horse was brought back to him. They had painted big white spots on him and added a fake mane and tail.

It was a cute story, but on several occasions during the road show we got a glitch in our computer and when Burt was talking about his beautiful blond wife, Loni, instead of her slide popping up on the laser disc, this horse with his painted spots and his fake mane and tail popped up.

Burt's one-man show was a hit with audiences in the twenty-three cities we toured; however, it was a financial failure.

Unfortunately, the marketing and promotion for the tour was not adequate for this type of show. When we arrived at the first couple of venues, we found a 1500- to 2000-seat house with 500 or more empty seats. We began calling local charitable groups and "papering" the house. Burt could not bear to see empty seats in the theatre. Sometimes in the midst of the show while a clip was on, he would step backstage and say to me, "There are five empty seats in row three, nine in row eighteen, and a dozen or more as far back as I can see."

I then had to leave my post at the computer, where I sat with the technician during the show, and go into the lobby to tell Lamar, who was setting up the T-shirts and souvenirs, to get people off the street, theatre ushers, anybody to fill those seats as soon as possible. I was used to this, because at Burt's theatre in Jupiter, he sat in his private box overlooking the audience, and if there were any empty seats, I had waiters and buspeople change into street clothes and sit in the seats.

The road show continued. When we arrived at a city, we immediately checked into a good hotel to shower and prepare for the night's performance. Burt and I went over the show schedule, he settled down to relax a little, and I joined the crew at the theatre, hall, or gym, wherever we were booked. When Burt arrived, I went into his dressing room to help him get his wardrobe together, assist him with his makeup, fix his hair (he always put on his hairpiece in the privacy of the bathroom, so I just glued the sides in place and combed it), and left him to get dressed. I then ran backstage to do a last-minute computer check with Dennis, our video technician.

The show began with a "clip tease," flashing slides of memorable pictures while "Dueling Banjos" from *Deliverance* was playing. At the last beat, Burt walked onstage and the crowd went crazy. They loved the stories, and Burt was such a good story-teller that he always received a standing ovation. When the show was over and we headed for the bus, there were always hundreds of fans waiting for an autograph, picture, or just a glimpse of him.

I remember one night during the road show as I was sitting with the technician at the computer backstage, Burt started talking about something we had not heard before. I usually was able to direct Dennis, the technician, to switch slides or the clip to where Burt had jumped in his stories, as I knew them so well. Not this time. He got louder and higher as he talked on and on and I thought, *Oh great, something's kicking in and God only knows where we go from here.*

It was near the end of the second act and Burt usually wore a big Hollywood hand-painted jeans jacket with rhinestones and glitz all over it. The audi-ence loved it when he walked onstage wearing it, and they screamed, whistled, and applauded loudly.

When the second act ended and he walked off-stage, I always met him and as we entered his dressing room, he handed me the jacket and went into the bathroom. As I started to hang the jacket up, I heard a rattling sound. I checked all of his pockets, but they were empty. Now this jeans jacket had no lining, but a very large hem. I ran my fingers along the bottom of the hemline and could feel a trail of pills inside. I opened the jacket and he had worked about a "hand-wide" opening in the hem so he could reach in and help himself every time a clip was running and it was dark on stage. I quickly removed the pills, all colors and sizes, not caring at the moment as to what they were, and not *daring* at the moment to confront him.

He was flying high by that time, but everything turned out fine.

When we did the show in Montgomery, Alabama, the venue was a huge gym. This particular show was a benefit for a hospital, and Burt had agreed to attend a cocktail party immediately after and schmooze. Therefore, the two-hundred center front seats were reserved for those special patrons who paid the big bucks to see the show and meet Burt afterwards. Curtain time came and all the seats were filled, with the exception of the two-hundred center front ones. Burt looked out and turned to me, "Where the hell is everybody?"

A few people started arriving and I went down to find out where the other one hundred and seventy-nine were. I was told that they were all at the pre-show cocktail party and many probably would not attend. I explained to the venue manager and the "benefit" woman that we had to fill the seats right away and start the show. I began inviting people in the surrounding seats to move up into the empty ones. The "benefit" lady, who was in charge, screamed at me, "You can't do that! These seats belong to doctors and lawyers and top business people here and they paid seventy-five dollars each for them. You can't bring people out of fifteen dollar seats to sit here!"

"Excuse me, but I certainly can. If those doctors, lawyers, and top business people had the courtesy to show up in time for the performance, they could have these seats; however, they have chosen not to do so and these other wonderful folks came early and now the show is twenty minutes late starting already. When the doctors, lawyers, and top business people arrive late, they can sit in the fifteen dollar vacant seats, quietly please, so as not to disturb the performance."

The big guy, who was manager of the building, also began screaming and told me that nobody was going to sit in those seats except the people who paid seventy-five dollars and if they didn't show, they'd stay empty!

"Fine," I said. "Why don't you explain that to Mr. Reynolds, who has been backstage waiting to go on for the last thirty minutes?"

"I sure as hell will!" he exclaimed. I turned to the $15 ticket holders who were waiting and told them to please fill the front seats. I turned to the two people in charge, who looked like they wanted to tear my head off, and politely said, "If Mr. Reynolds agrees with you, I'll be happy to come out here and remove every one of them."

"Ballistic" is a good description of Burt's response to the ". . . and I told her that those were important people who paid seventy-five dollars a piece for those seats!"

I really had to step in between them as Burt screamed, "I don't care if those ill-mannered, inconsiderate bastards paid a thousand dollars for a seat!" He continued to shout that he didn't want them in the theatre and that the only people he cared about were the ones in the audience now waiting for the show. He reduced "the big guy" to about three feet tall, and the "benefit" lady shriveled up to a whimpering puppy and came up to me and said, "I'm so sorry, I didn't realize he'd be so mad."

"Excuse me, lady, we have to start the show," I said, not even looking at her. After the show, we even went to the cocktail party because it was for the hospital, mingled with the slightly tipsy to knee-walking drunks for about fifteen minutes, and ran to the bus to "get the hell out of Dodge!"

Ironically, Burt and I both received a certificate from the governor's office declaring that we were now "Honorary Citizens of the State of Alabama."

Ken Kragen joined us during the tour and really made every effort to encourage sales and promotions. He is an extremely optimistic, high-energy, likeable guy. He explained that initially it appeared financially feasible to book the larger halls for one-night performances; however, in hindsight we should have booked smaller theatres for two or three nights. The primary question was, "What is Burt Reynolds going to do?" He was not known as a "song and dance" man, he didn't do Will Rogers or Mark Twain, so the promoters were having a tough time with marketing.

Ken then suggested that Burt do a few radio interviews when we arrived in each new town, so we set them up, carefully selecting the station and interviewer, so it kept the interviews to the issue of what the show was about and not about his personal life.

At one point in the tour, Ken met us backstage and Burt had become increasingly angry at the problem of empty seats. He screamed at Ken as if he were responsible (which was totally unjustified). Ken, realizing he could not resolve the situation to Burt's satisfaction, quietly left.

The following night after the performance, we were on the bus heading for the next town and Burt looked at me and said, "Where the hell was Kragen tonight? I never saw him."

"He's gone back to L.A., Boss. He faxed me his resignation today, but I didn't want to tell you until after the show."

"Well, that son of a bitch bailed out when the going got tough! Now what the hell are we going to do? Who is going to get word ahead and find out if they even know I'm coming?"

"Well, we've been in tight places before and we'll get out of this, or I'll call Lori (my daughter who was in Florida and formerly worked in public relations and marketing for Burt's theatre and the television series *B.L. Stryker*) and get her on it."

The next morning I called her with our dilemma, and when we stopped at the next town at a large truck stop to eat, she faxed layouts for newspaper ads. Burt approved them, and when we arrived in town, they were already in the paper and the theatre marquee read *"AN EVENING WITH BURT REYNOLDS* TONIGHT ONLY!"* According to the box-office staff, it paid off in sales that day. "How did you get that done so quickly?" I asked Lori. "Well, I promised the guy two free tickets and a visit backstage to personally meet Burt." She continued to market ahead of our tour, but by this point, we still ended up at a financial loss.

When I spoke with Ken Kragen back in Los Angeles, he said, "You know, Elaine, I really care about Burt, but he consumes you. I have a life outside of him with my other clients, and most importantly, my wife and my little girl."

God, I envied him. He's financially successful and a very happy and together person. He kept telling me, "All you can do, is all you can do, and all you can do is enough!" . . . But it never was enough for Burt. I always felt I had a bag of miracles I could reach into whenever I was in a jam, so I never had to disappoint him. My greatest fear was to one day reach into the bag . . . and it would be empty.

About halfway through the one-man show tour, Burt was on stage one night and as he began the first part of his show, which had to do with his early childhood, he stopped talking. He was on the story about his father coming home from the war and how big he seemed to him. He began again, and when he reached the story of how he "sassed" his mother and his father hit him so hard it knocked him into the closet and all the clothes fell down on him, he could hardly continue. He cut the first act short and Dennis, our video technician, and I followed the script as best we could and Burt walked off the stage with his head down. I followed him into his dressing room and asked what was wrong.

"I just realized something while I was out there. This is all about the fact that my father never told me he loved me!" he said, shaking his head.

"I knew that from the first show, Boss," I said. "You are still trying to get his approval and to get him to say, 'I love you!' "

Burt was so overwhelmed by this revelation, that he could hardly finish the show that night. I felt so sorry for him, because his father, mother, and sister never really were very demonstrative, and Burt hugs and kisses everybody. He almost became obsessed with the "my father never told me he loved me" syndrome, and he began to use it as an excuse every time he blew up on the set.

Once after a particularly bad week, Linda Bloodworth came to me and suggested, "Elaine, can't we just fly his father here, take Burt to the airport, let his Dad say 'I love you,' and hug him, and get back on the plane to Florida, so Burt can get on with the show?"

Burt always has to become the victim to excuse his behavior. Just once, I would have liked to have heard him admit, "I'm acting like a jerk because I'm spoiled and I want my way about everything!" Of course, he never will, and those around him will do as I did for many years, allow him to continue to get his way."

Governor Pete Wilson's Song and Dance

Burt never had a problem "blasting off" at the top executives of the networks or anyone on the set of one of his movies. However, Burt could never confront anyone close to him. If he recieved negative information about someone, he would hide away from them and never try to find out the truth. One of his former managers said to me, "Burt always believes the last guy who shook his hand." He just has one of his people tell them not to try and contact him anymore, and runs away allowing himself to become the victim.

A lot of good people have been caught in this trap and over the years he lost many loyal employees and friends. If at a later date, he found out that he made a mistake, he'd shake his head and say, "Damnit, I should have known better." But he never went back and told that person because he felt too guilty. He'll just wait a few years and contact them as if nothing ever happened.

Burt Sugarman, a very successful producer in Hollywood, contacted us about doing Burt's one-man show to benefit The Brain Tumor Research Center, University of California in San Francisco. Our tour had ended and we were looking forward to putting the show together again. This special benefit evening was a box-office sellout which pleased Burt to no end. However, about a week before the benefit show, we got word that a special "preshow" starring Mary Hart of *Entertainment Tonight* (and wife of Sugarman), Loni Anderson, and Lynda Carter was planned. As "a special treat," California governor Pete Wilson and his wife were also scheduled to do a song-and-dance number.

When Burt heard about this surprise preshow, he was angry about the idea, because it made his segment of the show run too late. To top it all off, we received a telephone call from an organizational head of the gay community in San Francisco, stating that if Governor Wilson performed, there would be a major disturbance at the theatre by a group of gay activists.

The problem stemmed from the fact that Governor Wilson had just vetoed an antidiscrimination bill which was important to the gay community (as well as other minorities), and it sent numerous groups into a frenzy all over the state. Burt was asked by representatives of the gay community to prevent the governor from performing. So I was told to call Bob Wynn, associate of Burt Sugarman and a producer on the benefit show, and tell him the governor could not perform on stage before Burt's show.

Well, I was told the governor was on the board of directors for the hospital and was Honorary Chairman for the benefit. Burt Sugarman and the rest of the events committee were quite incensed at "the Boss" for requesting this and refused to cancel the preshow. This really started a war and Burt refused to do his one-man show. It really got hot and heavy between them, and—as usual—I was the mediator, coupled with the task of dealing with the gay leaders as well.

An agreement was finally made that the governor would not appear on stage. I was associate producer on *Evening Shade* during this time as well, and after spending several late nights in the editing room with Burt and Tony Hayman, I was really exhausted. I found that this kind of stress can really cause your face to fall and you get old and ugly fast. I figured that If I ever stopped long enough to get a real face-lift, my eyes would literally be in the back of my head.

The big donors were treated to a black-tie dinner which was held in a very large tent adjacent to the theatre. Burt never made an appearance at the dinner, but Loni did. When the governor was introduced, everyone stood and applauded except Loni and Burt's people. Burt's show was ready to start on time; however, the entire group of people holding tickets for the orchestra seats were still under the "big tent." Burt sent me over to find out what the delay was and to tell Burt Sugarman that we had to start the show. When I entered the tent, Governor Wilson and his wife, Mary Hart, and Lynda Carter were doing their preshow presentation in the tent and not on the stage of the theatre as agreed. Caught in the crossfire, Loni had chosen not to perform at all.

Burt's entrance was delayed for forty-five minutes until the preshow was over. However, by the time he took the stage, he was so angry and completely unnerved that he gave the worst performance of the entire run of his one-man show. He refused to recognize the celebrities in the audience who had participated in the preshow, among others attending. This generated a lot of angry mail from people who demanded a refund because they bought tickets anticipating seeing so many celebrities, and they "only saw Burt Reynolds." Sadly, the respect and longtime friendship between Burt Reynolds and Burt Sugarman was more than strained.

Suzanne Somers

"Boss, do you want to do the Suzanne Somers show?" I asked. "The producer called today."

"No, I don't think so, I don't feel it's my kind of show or audience," he replied. However, Scott Jackson, Burt's assistant, received another call and the producers were really pushing to get Burt to do the show. Scott suggested he might want to do it based on the fact that Patrick Duffy would be on also.

I told Scott that I didn't feel that Burt should be doing these talk-shows so frequently. He had just previously done the Rick Dees show and Montel Williams. Burt was not happy with the outcome, but he finally agreed to do Suzanne's show anyway. I reminded Scott to make the producer aware of certain things Burt did not want to discuss: his nude layout in *Cosmopolitan*, the AIDS rumor, and anything else that had been "done to death" on talk shows. When we arrived at the studio, Burt found out that they wanted him to stretch out on a piano with Patrick Duffy while Suzanne sang

"Ain't Misbehavin' " Burt came over to me and said, "No way I'm doing that crap. I knew this was a mistake. I should have stuck with my first decision."

"Well, Boss, you can't leave now, so just go out there and be wonderful."

Suzanne's first remark to Burt was, "Well, I didn't recognize you with your clothes on," and she began to discuss his nude picture in *Cosmopolitan* almost twenty years earlier. She asked him about his relationship with Dinah. He spoke at length with such affection that he had me call Loni from the car after the show and tell her what a rotten time he had and that Dinah was the only thing he could talk about and stay calm. He was afraid she would be mad at him, because she was somewhat jealous of the close relationship he'd had with Dinah.

After I hung up the mobile phone, we continued to drive around for about an hour just looking at houses in the Los Feliz area. He pointed out some of the unique old homes where former great stars and producers had lived many years ago. It was therapeutic for him, and he finally settled down as we headed back to the office at the studio.

Caught!!

Late one morning, Scott Jackson came into my office and appeared to be rather upset. "Elaine, the *Enquirer* is going to break the story about Burt putting Pam up at the Radisson Bel-Air and I don't know how to stop it."

"How did they find out she was there? You did register in your name, didn't you?"

"Yes, but I think I screwed up. On the registration slip, it asked the name of the other person in the room. I didn't think and put Pam's name there," he said. "Burt's going to kill me. I can't take this kind of stress."

"Well, Lamar has always handled this, and this is your first time, but you've got to be careful," I said. I felt badly for Scott, because I knew he was going to face a lot of similar situations while doing his job.

It took the tabloids about thirty minutes to put that one together. They had been aware of Burt and Pam's relationship for some time, but were trying to get some concrete evidence. Their contacts on the East coast were always on the alert. If Pam was not at her job at Mahlio's Restaurant in Tampa, Florida, they assumed she was with Burt in California.

Scott, of course, did not spend the night at the hotel, and when Pam put on her running clothes the next morning, she told me a guy was right in front of her door, squatting down as if to scrape gum or something off the carpet. She said that she looked down, but did not see anything on the rug, and felt a little uneasy. However, she continued down the hall to the outside and turned back, and the guy was watching her.

After her morning run and she came back to her room, a towel that had been in the bathroom was now on a chair and her bags had been moved a little. She had luggage tags with her address in Lutz (the town just outside of Tampa, Florida, where she lived). So the fun began. Scott received a call from a tabloid and when he insisted Pam was visiting with him he was told that they had already checked it out and they knew it was not true. They insisted she was here for Burt, so Scott asked what Burt could do to kill the story and was told the only way, was to give them a better story.

"No way," I said. "Burt would never tell them anything. You know how he hates those sheets."

"Well, he has to this time, or they're going to expose him." Scott was truly frightened. "The desk clerk told me he got a call from Burt's business manager in Florida inquiring if Pam Seals was registered and if so, to send the bill to him."

"Well, I know that's not true, it had to be one of the tabloids. They are really clever."

"Please don't tell Burt I did that, he'll fire me," Scott begged.

"There is no reason to, what's done is done. I'm sure you won't make the same mistake again, but you're going to have to talk to him about this. I'm tied up with the show. Dive in and just tell him, it'll get worked out."

Later Scott came to me and said, "I know you don't agree, but he has decided to give them a story, probably the one about his losing so much money in bad business ventures or something like that. Also, they'll pay him well for an exclusive interview."

"Hey, It's his life, not mine," I replied.

It's Only a Slide Show

An Evening with Burt Reynolds, was rather expensive to produce when he performed using the laser disc with film clips and full crew, so we trimmed it down to where Burt could basically do the show with a few of the stories and slides.

In 1992 Doug McClure had become the national in-house celebrity for a marketing firm that was interested in having Burt perform his one-man show at conventions and sales promotional meetings for a large food company all over the country. As it turned out, it was a very profitable situation for Burt. Wherever we went, the stage crew for the sales meetings already had the sound and lighting systems up and we shipped them the furnishings for the show. They set that up and we just showed up with Burt, a few slides, and a cassette tape with the intro music.

Scott went with us so he could learn to do the show and to take care of Burt. We had simplified the format so much that an orangutan could run the show if he could just stay three steps ahead of Burt.

At one venue, we were in a huge convention hall and the projectionist, for some reason or other, was mounted on top of a fifty-foot-high platform. Usually, I stood next to the guy, so that when Burt would skip a story or forget where he was, I could cue the operator as to how to pick it up or cover it. Scott was learning the show, but he had a tendency to panic when something went wrong.

The technician was sitting on a rather makeshift platform of plywood on top of scaffolding with hardly room for one body, so in this particular situation, I decided that I wouldn't sit with him. Besides I have had vertigo for over ten years and wouldn't be much use up there.

Or so I thought.

Everything started to fall apart. Burt was already in a bad mood before we began and was having trouble remembering the stories. His knee gave out, the guy running the slide projector from his "squirrel's perch" had no clue as to what was happening on stage, and Burt was starting to panic.

I turned to Scott and said, "Get up there on the platform and just follow my lead. I'll coach Burt from stage left, so just watch me."

"I'm not going up on that rickety thing, besides I don't know what to do when I get up there!" he said.

"For God's sake, Scott, I'll never make it. There's not even a ladder, just the crossbars on

the scaffold!" One look at his face and I knew I
had to do it.

It was a tough job, but somebody had to do
it . . . and my job was to always "save" Burt.

I ran over to the scaffold and never looked down.
I must have looked like a monkey scrambling up
the side of that thing. Burt was in the middle of
a particular story and the slide was about a different one. I had the technician switch over and we
got him back on track and finished the show. The
lights came on and Scott met Burt at the edge of
the stage and put his arm around him for support,
and Burt headed for the dressing room.

As they passed under the scaffolding, I said,
"Hi, Boss! You came through that one okay. I'll
meet you guys in the dressing room as soon as I
figure out how I'm going to get down."

"Okay, honey, thanks a lot," Burt said as he hob-
bled off.

The technician was already down on the floor
and continuing his job of assisting in striking (re-
moving) the set. As I sat on the plywood platform,
the crew was bustling about and I called down,
"Hey, guys, can I get a little help to get down? Uh,
I've got a plane to catch!" But I didn't seem to get
anyone's attention and every time I looked down,
I panicked.

Once I even lay down on my stomach and wrig-
gled over to the edge and tried to find something
to support my foot, but the crisscrossed pipes didn't
offer anything but air!

Finally, a guy on a forklift passed underneath me.

"HELP!" I screamed as loudly as possible to be heard above the noise of moving furniture and rolling speakers and everything else going on below.

The driver of the forklift looked up and said, "Need some help down, little lady?"

No thanks, I felt like saying, *I'm just up here trying to get closer to God!* But I didn't. "Please get me down and I'll pray for you, your wife, and your kids for the rest of my life!"

"Be right back," he said and left. He returned, raising a platform with a railing around it and I gingerly stepped over on to it. He lowered me to the floor and I headed for the dressing room.

When I walked in, Burt looked at me and said, "We're ready to go. Where've you been?"

"Gee, Boss, I'm sorry. I was just over talking with the crew!"

The Fistfight

"What the hell's going on over there, Elaine?!" Harry Thomason's voice rang out over the phone. "I'm in my car on the way in for the read-through and I just got a call from the office saying 'Burt's canceled the read-through because he didn't like the script.' Well, it's a heckuva time to let everybody know after they've all come in to work. He got the script last night before everybody else, why didn't he call somebody then? Frankly, I'm sick and tired of him being so inconsiderate. As a courtesy he could have at least called me. I am supposed to be an executive producer, and I'm the last to know. Is he in his office now? He's been wanting a fistfight with me, so now he can have it. Tell him to meet me in the parking lot right now, and we'll settle this once and for all!" God, he was livid.

"Harry," I said, "I just found out about it, so I don't know whether he asked someone else to call you first or not. He's not looking for a fistfight and besides you guys can't settle this in front of the cast and crew. So please just go on to your office and I'll find out what happened and I'll call you as soon as I talk with him."

"Okay," Harry replied, "but Linda and I are not going to keep putting up with him doing things like this all the time."

"Boss," I said to Burt as I entered his office adjacent to mine, "Harry just called from his car on the way in to the office and wants to know why the read-through was canceled."

"Because the script sucks!" Burt yelled back at me. It didn't help that it was written by one of the guys on staff whose writing Burt didn't like anyway. "Why? Does he have a problem with that? Because if he does he can just come up here and say it to my face!"

"Boss," I lied, "he's not mad. He just wanted to know why you didn't call him first before canceling the read-through, so that since everyone had come in this morning, maybe the two of you might have decided to do the read-through and explain to everyone that there would be some major changes. By the time his office called him on his mobile phone, everyone had been dismissed."

"To Hell with him, if he thinks this piece of shit deserves to be read, let him take it over to *Designing Women* and let them read it!" he responded.

"Boss," I lied again, "I told you he's not upset, so you don't have to be either." Burt can be reasoned with even when he's mad, and especially if he's wrong. "Why don't you just apologize for not calling him first. You would be furious with him if he did that to you," I said calmly. "He just wants to talk to you about why you hate the script so much. He should be in his office now. Can I call him for you?"

Burt looked at me with that raised-eyebrow expression of his and said, "Okay, but he better not come looking for a fight, or he'll get one!"

"Harry," I said when he answered his phone. "I just talked to Burt and he wants you to come to his office to discuss the script."

"Is he screaming and yelling, because if he is, I'm not going up there and deal with that," Harry said.

"No," I said, lying again. "He's not upset, he realizes that he should have talked with you about it first, but he just got angry and made a snap decision. He knows that he would not have liked you doing that to him either."

"Okay," Harry said, "I'll be up there in a few minutes. I have to make one call first."

When Harry came upstairs to Burt's office, he went in and closed the door. Two of the guys in the office stood with their ears to the door and listened. A few times voices were raised enough for me to hear in my office next door. When it finally calmed down and they came into the outer office, they gave each other a hug, and Harry headed back downstairs.

"Blessed are the peacemakers," I could hear my mama's voice, "for they shall inherit the earth."

You Oughta Be in Pictures

"When we get this last cut done, can you stay a little longer and help me? I've got some new pictures to put up in my dressing room," Burt asked as we sat in the editing room. It was already close to midnight and he was still going strong.

"Okay, but where are you going to put them?" I asked. I knew there were autographed photos from his celebrity friends from the floor to the ceiling on every wall in his office, my office, his dressing room, and just about everywhere in the building except Jerry Seinfeld's office below us.

"I'm going to rearrange the ones in my dressing room so I can hang them in there," he said.

Burt was taking a lot of Didrex, a diet pill that gives you an overabundance of energy when taken in large quantities as Burt did; it can keep you up day and night, but dangerously on edge.

When he mentioned hanging pictures, I knew it was for the rest of the night. Fortunately, after Scott Jackson took over some of my duties, he got to spend the night with the Boss holding the hammer and nails.

Burt shipped copies of these pictures to Valhalla, his home in Jupiter, the offices at his ranch, the tack store, and his parents' home. We had them in the theatre, the rehearsal hall, plus The Backstage, his restaurant in Jupiter, and Burt and Jack's, his restaurant in Ft. Lauderdale, Florida. When he still owned Reynolds Plaza, they were all over the offices there also.

A few years ago he had condominiums on the east coast of Florida in Pompano Beach and Miami, and in Indian River Shores on the west coast of Florida. These condos were provided for his use in the event he had reason to be in the area, plus the sales staff could tell prospective buyers that Burt Reynolds "lived" there. And yes, these same pictures were in these places as well.

When we first moved into our new offices to begin production of *Evening Shade,* Burt not only filled his, mine, and Lamar's offices with these pictures, but put them up in Linda and Harry's offices as well. When the Thomasons came in the next morning, they removed them and said thank you, but they really had planned to just hang a few of their own pictures and some special paintings.

Burt was a bit chagrined. He felt they were ungrateful and said, "To hell with them. I won't do anything for them again!" These photographs were so important to him that he just took for granted that anyone would be thrilled to have pictures of these legendary celebrities around them.

Burt was obsessed with these photographs. He constantly shipped large boxes filled with pictures back and forth across the country.

I used to tell him, "Boss, don't send any more pictures, please send some more walls!"

He'd just laugh and say, "That's okay, we'll take some down and hang the new ones up when I get there."

Somehow, I always felt that Burt, not feeling loved by his own family, had created a false sense of love and adoration by surrounding himself with pictures of all the "important people" who had passed through his life. By having them on display at every place he went, that feeling of "somebody loves me" lifted his spirits and his self-esteem.

Burt's Near Tragedy

"My God, he's on fire!" I heard someone yell. I was sitting upstairs in the audience next to Loni on the set of *Evening Shade*. In this particular episode, Burt and Michael Jeter were on a road trip in a small camper. The scene had Burt cooking and a small flash fire develops. Michael comes out spraying everything with a fire extinguisher. The fire extinguisher was filled with baby powder and had worked fine in a demonstration earlier in the parking lot. However, the baby powder used on the set contained cornstarch, which is highly flammable. When the powder hit the flame, all the dust exploded into flames.

Fortunately, Burt's hands were covered with a flame-retardant gel and with his past experience of being set on fire for a movie, he instinctively fell to the floor and rolled to put out the flames. Loni and I ran on to the set and the paramedics were called. Burt was examined and he insisted on reconstructing the stove and continuing to film. The paramedics were trying to get him to go to the burn center for examination of his lungs. He sent them away and Loni went outside to talk with them. I called his personal physician and asked that he come over to examine Burt anyway. I then walked outside with Loni. "He has to go to the hospital to have his lungs checked. They said he ingested the chemicals from the burning powder and could develop a major respiratory problem," she said.

"You have to convince him to go. If I go up on the set he'll probably yell at me in front of everybody and it's too embarrassing," Loni said to me as we walked back to the set. As I walked into the camper, his longtime director-friend Tony Wharmby was standing outside. "You must get him to go to the hospital, Elaine, he has breathed in those fumes and he could die!"

Loni stood at the door of the camper watching as I approached Burt. He looked up at me and said angrily, "I'm not going anywhere, I'm fine!" He coughed a few times as he spoke.

"You are not," I said firmly. "The paramedics said you could die within twenty-four hours with that chemical stuff in your lungs, so you have to go, Boss. I'll explain to the audience that you're going to the emergency room for a quick checkup and will be back to finish the show. We'll serve them coffee and snacks from craft services if they want to stay, and if you have to stay overnight, I'll call from the hospital and they can go home."

We checked him into the hospital and Loni stayed with him when we left. John and Janet came with Quinton so he could visit his dad and to eventually take Loni home. He stayed a couple of days for observation and when he came back to the office, he wanted to make a statement to the press about the danger of baby powder with cornstarch around an open flame. I purchased several brands of baby powder, some with cornstarch and some without. Those without did not ignite when we shook it in front of a match; the ones with cornstarch literally blew up. Burt was really concerned that children Quinton's age could actually shake the can of baby powder containing cornstarch in front of an open flame, like a fireplace or someone striking a match to light a cigarette, and it would ignite.

Television news cameras filmed Burt explaining what had happened on the set and showed the actual film of him going up in flames. It was a frightening experience, but he turned it into a very important safety message to parents of small children.

Promises! Promises!

"Folks, I'd like to introduce the next mayor of Evening Shade!" Burt announced at the wrap party for the 1991-92 season of *Evening Shade*. A grinning George Lindsey, who played Goober for many years on *The Andy Griffith Show*, joined Burt on stage. He joked and entertained the cast, crew, and their families as we celebrated the end of another season of the show. When Burt finished and came off the stage, George came over to me and said, "Well, I never expected that, but I sure am thrilled. I'll call my agent tomorrow and he can get in touch with you to follow up on this and rearrange my schedule."

Actually, it came as a surprise to everyone, including Linda Bloodworth-Thomason, the creator of *Evening Shade*. George left the party elated at the possibility of being cast in another hit television series. Unfortunately, Burt was famous for making promises to people and later either changing his mind, or being unable to fulfill his promises, or forgetting he ever made the promise. George never even got to do one show, much less become a regular on the series.

I had known that James Hampton, who is one of the funniest people on earth, and Burt were friends for over twenty years. During the first ten years or so of my relationship with Burt, oddly enough, I never saw him. I met most of Burt's close friends, because he'd have them come to the theatre at one time or another during the ten years he owned it. Jim was the bugler on *F Troop* for many years, and co-starred with Burt in *Fade-In* in 1968 and in 1974 played his buddy in prison in *The Longest Yard*.

During the first season of *Evening Shade* Burt was less than enamored with the writers of the show with the exception of Linda Bloodworth-Thomason. He was constantly complaining about the scripts the writers were presenting. Linda had her hands full with *Designing Women* at that time, so, of course, she couldn't write every one of them. After the Monday morning read-through of each week's show, Burt would take the writers on staff into a room and basically rewrite the whole episode. This, of course, kept the morale pretty low among the creative team.

In one particular episode, the script included two of Wood Newton's old buddies. Doug McClure was cast in one part and suggested Jim Hampton for the other buddy. Now Burt had not spoken to Jim for twelve years at this time; however, recognizing that the character was a definite Hampton part, he thought it was a great idea. When Jim came on the set, Burt greeted him as if they had seen each other every day for the past twelve years. Jim came in and not only performed, but tactfully suggested some really funny lines that reminded Burt that his old buddy would be an asset to this show. Burt suggested to Linda and Harry that they hire him as a writer on the show. They knew him as an actor, but not a writer so they were a little skeptical. However, after meeting him and reading some of his work, they immediately hired him. Jim was a producer/writer on *Evening Shade* until its cancellation and has become a successful director in his own right.

When Jim first arrived I asked him why I had never met him before, considering Burt had always spoken so highly of him. He told me that he and Burt had been close buddies for many years and after *The Longest Yard* and *W.W. and the Dixie Dancekings,* Burt was preparing to film *Gator* and promised him the role of the F.B.I. agent. This film was to be Burt's directing debut, so he told Jim he definitely had the part.

Jim had just been nominated for a Golden Globe Award, and it appeared his career was off and running. However, when Jim's agent Larry Kubik called and told him the producers wanted to meet with him, Jim was elated and rushed over to finalize the deal. Jim said that as he sat in the meeting, he began to realize that the "deal" as he saw it was not the one he had been promised, and in fact, as someone put it, "Burt wants you to take his place, so he can go over and look behind the camera and make sure the shot is right."

"Wait a minute," Jim said. "Do you mean I'm to be his 'stand-in?' [This requires nothing but a body to mark the spot for filming.] I have to talk with Burt. There has been some mistake."

He tried to call Burt, but did not hear back from him. He called Larry, his agent, and asked, "What should I do? I can't believe Burt would do this to me. I know we're friends, but I don't feel I can just be his stand-in, yet I don't want to make Burt mad at me."

"Well," Larry told him, "if you feel guilty enough to do it, you don't need an agent, so save your money."

Jim didn't do the stand-in part, and Burt didn't speak to him for over twelve years. He said that he was watching a talk-show one night shortly after his meeting with the producers on that fateful day and Norman Fell was on the show. When he was asked what his next project was going to be, he said, "Well, Burt Reynolds had promised me a juicy role as an F.B.I. agent in his next film *Gator,* but he gave it to Jack Weston instead!"

Truthfully, Burt often makes these promises with earnest intentions, but if he is unable to fulfill them, he simply drops the whole issue without an explanation at all.

Commercially Speaking

"Well, I'm not crazy about the idea of doing commercials, but I need the money," Burt said to me one day in 1991. "At least this one won't be shown In the United States. It's for British Petroleum and will only play in Europe."

I received a call a few days later from the casting agency. The commercial was to be filmed in Los Angeles on the lot of one of the main studios. As we approached the filming date, Burt became more and more agitated at having committed to doing the commercial. I kept reminding him that the money was good and that it would not be seen here in the States. Besides, a lot of major stars do foreign commercials just for the money.

The morning of the shoot, I arrived on the set before him. I checked his dressing-room trailer, located just outside of the sound stage where the filming would take place, to make sure it had the usual supply of water, iced tea with at least fifty packets of Equal (he puts six packets in each glass of tea), fruit, cheese and crackers to combat his hypoglycemia. Setting the stage for Burt's arrival, I walked around the set and introduced myself to the producer, director, and crew members.

He arrived "as nervous as a whore in church," as we used to say. He was irritated at everything, but tried to mask it by making funny—yet sometimes too curt—remarks about everything.

It's gonna be a long day, I thought to myself, *and full of fireworks!*

The director, an Englishman with excellent credentials, came in to Burt's dressing room and began to discuss how they were going to shoot the commercial.

He listened and was polite, and as soon as the director left, Burt said to me, "Let's just get this over and get the hell out of here. I wish I'd never said I would do this. I absolutely hate it!"

"It should be fairly easy and I've already met the crew. They are very professional and seem pretty warm, so that always helps," I said.

Burt was to play a suave, Cary Grant-type character in a romantic setting in front of a fireplace. He was drinking a glass of champagne and he was touting the merits of this "petrol."

Burt always has a little trouble taking direction. For one thing, he has in his mind already what to do and where to stand for the cameras, so when he's told to do something else, he has a tendency to balk. Each time the director changed something or corrected something, Burt visibly became more agitated.

His whole demeanor was changing rapidly. I was

beginning to notice definite mood swings and it was making me more than a little nervous. I knew he wasn't going to make it without blowing up.

Each time we took a break, I tried to settle him down. He slammed things around in his dressing room and yelled, then settled down and went back to the set.

As the day labored on, he became more arrogant and flippant on the set. At one point, the four people from British Petroleum motioned for the director to come over to them. They had a suggestion and when the director came over to Burt to change something, Burt blew up and started yelling at the director in front of the crew and the officials from British Petroleum. The director, who had been the brunt of Burt's sarcasm all day, came back with a few choice words. That did it! Burt went ballistic and the director realized how totally out of control Burt was, so he insisted they finish the discussion in the parking lot. Burt's anger was unbelievable and he thought the director was looking for a fight as they went outside.

The crew took a break and sat down. I apologized to everyone and made an excuse for Burt's behavior and hurried to the parking lot to "pick up the remains of the loser." The two of them were yelling at each other, so I didn't interrupt. Burt glanced over at me, but kept right on yelling.

I walked back onto the soundstage and as I approached the crew, everyone stopped talking and looked up as if I was going to make some grand statement like, *It was a draw. They're both dead,* or

Pack up, it's a wrap for today, or *We aren't going to finish this commercial, so go home, your check is in the mail.* However, being of unsound mind and—thank God—a sound body, instead I announced, "They're still discussing the lighting and asked that I entertain you folks until they resolve the situation." I then broke into a tap dance, singing "There's No Business Like Show Business!" Everyone laughed and relaxed and started moving onto the set.

I walked back outside and over to the two men, who were now just having a slightly heated discussion. I stood looking at them and smiling. Burt reached over and put his arm around me and pulled me over to them.

"We've got it all straightened out now. Tell the crew we're coming in," Burt said.

"You've got it!" I replied and started walking toward the soundstage.

We finished the commercial and Burt left the set vowing, "Elaine, that's the last fucking commercial I'm ever going to do!" When the check arrived, he must have changed his mind.

"Quaker State, the oil company, is going to pay me a million dollars to do a commercial for them," Burt said to me several months later. "You'll get a call from their advertising guy in the next few days, so get all the details for me. I told them I'd do it if we could film it at my ranch while we are in Florida and they agreed."

Oh, boy, here we go again! I thought.

"This one will be more fun because it will be done at the ranch and it'll be a lot more relaxed.

They're sending a script right away, so when it comes, bring it in my office and we'll work on it." Burt appeared to be a little more excited over this one than the last—of course, it was a lot more money, too.

When the script came, Burt took one look at it and said, "I'm not saying this crap. Here, sit down with me and we'll write a new one. In the first place, they've got me holding up a can of oil like I'm some junk-yard mechanic and giving a direct pitch. I'm not going to do that!"

He began to rewrite the entire commercial. When it was returned to the Quaker State folks, they rejected it and went back to the original idea. Well, that set off the first bomb.

George Newell, who has been with Grey Advertising in New York for many years, is one of the nicest guys to work with. He has a great sense of humor and is really accommodating, yet gets the job done.

But Burt was now in charge. It was going to be *his* commercial about whatever *he* chose to say, and *he* was going to direct it and *he* was going to star in it. Without going into all of the gory details, I felt like a volleyball . . . back and forth . . . back and forth . . . between Burt and the Quaker State team. There were four regulars on the Quaker State team and only one of Burt; however, he began acting like an eighteen-hundred-pound gorilla, so he didn't need any other team members.

We finally worked things out and filming began. I had to leave just before the last day of shooting to go to Tampa and search for a house to lease for Burt during the filming of *Cop and a Half* and to get ready for the picture. I turned to Scott Jackson, his assistant, and said, "I'm outta here. It's your turn to watch him!"

Cop and a Half

"Elaine, we have to try and get this movie for Burt." It was Andrea Eastman, Burt's agent with ICM in New York "The script is perfect for him and he really needs a movie."

"Great! What do you need to help lock it in?" I asked.

"Well, truthfully, Henry Winkler is directing it and Imagine and Universal are producing it with Paul Maslansky. The problem is that they are really trying to get James Caan. But Henry keeps insisting that Burt would be wonderful and wants to direct him in it."

"So, what's it about?" I asked.

"A cop and a small kid who wants to be a cop."

"That's perfect for Burt. He really is great with kids," I offered.

"I know that, but they don't, so I'll keep you posted."

"Well, if you talk to Burt about it, don't tell him they want Caan or he won't do it anyway."

A couple of weeks later, she called again. "Jimmy

Caan passed and now they are trying to get Sean Connery."

"Oh for gosh sakes, I like both of those guys, but Burt will be better. He was so good when he cohosted the People's Choice Awards with Macaulay Culkin last year. Maybe I can get a clip and send it so you can show them the interaction. Also, when we auditioned little kids for *Evening Shade*, Burt was terrific with Jacob Parker, the little boy from Dallas, Texas, who we cast. I think I can get a copy of that also. When they see him with these kids, they'll want him for sure."

Several weeks later, she phoned me back and announced, "You were right, Elaine, the clips were great and they're going to sign Burt. Thanks so much, you're the greatest." Andrea was delighted.

When we had the final callbacks of five kids for the costarring role in *Cop and a Half*, they were held on the set of *Evening Shade* for Burt's convenience. Representatives from Universal Studios, Imagine Films (Ron Howard's production company), Paul Maslansky, the producer, and Henry Winkler, the director, were all present.

After the first three kids auditioned, Burt stormed out and began yelling at Henry Winkler. "I thought you said two or three thousand kids were auditioned for this part all over the country! Where the hell did these come from? If they are the finalists, the other two thousand nine hundred and ninety-five must have been terrible!"

When Henry tried to explain to him, Burt just grew more angry and yelled obscenities at Henry. Paul Maslansky was standing there and said, "Just a minute, Burt, don't talk to our director like that!"

Burt turned to Paul and screamed, "Fuck you! I'll knock you over that fence if you say another word!"

"Boss!" I yelled as I grabbed him by the arm, "There are two little kids just over there waiting to audition and they can see and hear you!" He turned and when he saw them, he smiled and waved and said "Hi!" and went back inside to finish the auditions.

Henry was devastated, and I thought, *God, Henry is one of the nicest men in this business and he certainly didn't deserve that!* Henry turned and went back inside.

Paul Maslansky is a big guy over six feet tall who is tough, yet gentle, and a very good producer. He has produced all of the *Police Academy* films as well as over fifty more successful ones. He was angry! He left the set and I walked over to the offices across the street with him. "This is never going to work. I had no idea Burt was like this. I had heard he had a temper, but I gave him the benefit of the doubt. I just wanted to have fun making a good picture. He acts like he's on some kind of drugs or something. He is totally out of control." Paul shook his head and said, "I just don't know what to do."

I went back into the office with him and we sat with the producer from Imagine. I began to make excuses for Burt's action. After a few minutes, Scott came in and said, "Burt's found the kid. He wants you to come back over and see him." Eight-year-old Norman Golden II was, without a doubt, a hit with all of us. Very talented, very bright, and wise beyond his years. With all of the production people finally in agreement, everyone settled down and began to concentrate on making the movie.

I was responsible for finding a house for Burt to live in while filming *Cop and a Half* in Tampa. I contacted Toni Everett, one of the top Real Estate brokers in Florida. Toni managed to convince people to move out of their own mansions for that period of time if their house was selected by "this mystery V.I.P." who was coming to town. It was common knowledge around town that Burt Reynolds and Henry Winkler were coming to do a film, and I'm sure they hoped one of them was the V.I.P. and would stay in their house. It's amazing what celebrity status can do.

Toni drove me across the bay to Clearwater, and located right on the water was a very attractive contemporary house in a gated community. It was perfect, so she talked the owner into moving out for three months and Burt moved in.

Scott Jackson, Burt's assistant, and Howard Sussman, his dresser from *Evening Shade*, moved into the house with him.

Scott's duties were to keep Burt apprised of his shooting schedule and make sure he was available at all times in case Burt needed anything. Howard arranged for Burt's tailor to do the fitting and proceeded to order custom-made sport jackets at $1700 each, not only for Burt, but for his stand-in and photo double as well, a total of ten jackets at $17,000. The unit production manager and Paul Maslansky went ballistic.

When Paul called me about it, I immediately called Howard. I explained to him that I had to tell Burt, because it would certainly be brought to his attention later.

Howard was upset with me, but I had no choice. When I had an opportunity to talk with Burt about it, he said, "Well, I guess he didn't know any better. It's his first movie, but he should have asked somebody first, but tell Maslansky that I'll pay for them."

During the filming of *Cop and a Half*, Burt gave Henry Winkler a hard time about his directing. Every time Burt treated Henry badly, I wanted to tell him, "He's the only one who wanted you," but then I knew he'd be angry at Paul and all the other producers. It would only make things worse.

One day he was being particularly difficult and yelled in anger, "To hell with all of them, if they don't like what I'm doing, tell them to go get Jimmy Caan!"

I really wanted to yell back, *That's who they wanted in the first place and he passed!!*

* * *

I flew to Tampa, Florida, a couple of weeks ahead of Burt to participate in the preproduction of *Cop and a Half*. Henry Winkler, Paul Maslansky, and I had such fun casting the rest of the film. There was a lot of laughter and play, along with serious business surrounding the excitement of getting ready to begin filming. A few days prior to Burt's arrival, I toured the sets created for the film. Burt's character was "Nick," and his apartment was filled with baseball memorabilia. I spoke to the set designer. "This is all wonderful; however, Burt is such a football fan, he is going to want all of this changed to FSU memorabilia, I'm sure."

"Well," she said, "the script calls for Nick to be a big baseball fan, and it might be better if it doesn't identify with Burt Reynolds. I think we will leave it for him to see and hopefully he will be receptive."

"Well," I remarked, "I don't think he will, and it might be a good idea for you to start collecting FSU items as a backup before he gets here."

Sure enough, Burt's first day of walking the set, he looked at me and said, "What the hell is all this baseball crap doing in my apartment? Didn't you tell them that I love football, not baseball?"

"Yes, Boss, I did," I replied, "but Nick loves baseball."

"I don't care. I'm Nick, aren't I, and this Nick likes football!" he said. The set designer quickly replied to him, "Oh, it's no problem, we'll change it right away to football."

The filming of *Cop and a Half* was rather unpleasant every day. Burt was very unhappy that Henry Winkler was directing and continually chided him in front of the crew. Henry was making every effort to direct the movie without upsetting Burt, yet it didn't seem to matter. Paul Maslansky was beside himself. He came to me constantly and vented his anger at the way Burt conducted himself on the set. He kept saying, "I just wanted to have fun making this movie, but it's impossible"

Once we were shooting a street scene in Tampa and it was hot and humid. There were probably one hundred or more spectators standing outside the boundaries watching the filming. Burt was in a particularly bad mood, having just returned from his mother's funeral in Jupiter earlier that week. The first A.D. (assistant director) called to start rolling, when the second A.D. came forward with a question. The First A.D., recognizing the circumstances of the star, insisted on continuing. The second A.D. said, "Yeah, but wait a minute," and began to ask his question anyway.

Burt turned and started toward the second A.D. with fire in his eyes and began lashing out at him. The A.D. backed up, but kept saying something like, "Wait a minute, what's the problem, I'm just trying to explain . . ." I realized that Burt was becoming more aggressive and still screaming at the A.D., and no one was making a move. Scott—who is about six feet five inches tall—was frozen. Brian McManus, his hair and makeup guy, who works out and rides a motorcycle, just stood there.

My God, I thought, *he's going to hit him!* I began to move toward Burt and as I reached him, I grabbed his arm and said, "Stop it, Boss. Everybody's watching you!"

He jerked his arm free and yelled "NO!" and turned back to the A.D. and screamed, "My mother just died!" and placed his hands up toward the A.D.'s chest as the A.D. tripped on an uneven brick in the pavement and fell down.

"It's not his fault your mother died, now go to the bus!" I told him through clenched teeth.

About that time, Brian rushed over to grab Burt's other arm and pulled him away. I helped the A.D. up and told him to go to his trailer and I'd be right there.

"I don't understand," he said. "I was just trying to explain what I said."

"It doesn't matter when he's like this, it's better not to try to tell him anything," I said as he walked off the set. I went over to the camera where Burt was standing with Henry. He was very upset and Henry was explaining to Burt that he would talk with the A.D. and settle things down.

"No," Burt said, "let Elaine do it, she can straighten it out."

"Go to the bus, Boss. Henry and I both will talk with him and I'll be over there soon."

Henry and I talked with the A.D. and although

he was devastated, he accepted the funeral excuse and was willing to forget it and go back to work.

I then went back over to Burt's bus and he was lying on his bed in the back, crying. "It's okay, Boss, but you've gotta stop losing it no matter what's bothering you, especially in front of the crew and fans." I felt like I was talking with my son.

When the movie finally wrapped, the crew presented me with an official referee's uniform, whistle and all!

After the altercation Burt had with the second A.D. we were preparing to resume filming. Burt and Norman were waiting to begin the car scene. Those of us wearing headsets could overhear the conversation in the car between Norman and Burt.

"You shouldn't have done that to Glen back there, you know," Norman said.

"Do you think I was wrong?" Burt asked.

"Yeah, especially in front of everybody like that," Norman said.

"I guess you're right," said Burt. "I just lost my temper."

Norman is from a very fine family, and his mother, Theresa, and I became good friends during the film and continue to be so. She and her husband had a real concern for Norman's welfare and were very protective. Once she said to me, "I wish all these people wouldn't tell Norman how much they 'love' him and that when they get back to L.A. they're going to be doing all kinds of things together. I know full well it's not true and that they don't mean it."

"No, that isn't necessarily so, Theresa, they are sincere . . . for the moment . . . and I really mean that. The problem is, that when they do get back to Los Angeles, they get so busy trying to find the next job that they won't think about it. If they happen to work with him again on another film, it will be just like yesterday and they will pick up where they left off. That's just the way it works in this business."

When I came back to Los Angeles and settled in, I called Theresa to see how Norman was doing. This had been his first film; being a costar, he was catered to by everyone around him for three months. He had to feel a tremendous void, and I knew it would be difficult for him to settle back into his former lifestyle. Theresa said to me, "You know, Elaine, you and Henry Winkler are the only ones who have called to even ask about Norman. Burt hasn't called at all, and Norman is really hurt. He keeps saying, 'Burt said he was my friend, why doesn't he call me?' "

"I don't understand it," she said. "He doted on Norman all summer long, bought him presents, had us out to his ranch and house in Jupiter, and promised Norman they would see each other when he got back to Los Angeles. Why do you think he would make a promise to Norman like that and then not call?"

"I don't know, Theresa, I guess he's just busy with *Evening Shade*," I said.

When we shot *Cop and a Half*, Burt decided he didn't like the opening sequence Universal was planning on using to run behind the titles. So he flew cinematographer Nicky McLean in from Los Angeles and utilizing some of the film crew, created an opening scene from a helicopter that he felt was much more effective.

It never dawned on Burt that everyone was not going to be overwhelmed. He honestly felt that his choice of scenes was much better than those selected by Universal. He was anxious to show his footage to Paul Maslansky, Henry Winkler, and Tova Leiter, who was with Imagine Productions.

He was very proud of the footage they had filmed and sat down with me in the editing room, giving me notes as to the exact moment he wanted a particular scene to begin and end.

I took his notes and all the film footage over to Clearwater to Stuart Arnold's CPN Studios to edit, mix in the musical background, and have it back by 7:00 P.M. to run after dailies (the film footage shot the day before).

When I showed him the cut I'd made, he hugged me and said, "It's perfect. You're a better producer than any of those guys back in L.A."

"Thanks, Boss. I'm glad you're happy with it. I loved doing it," I said. However, Universal chose to stay with their own opening shots and all the extra money spent to produce Burt's proposed opening shots was wasted.

When we filmed the barroom-brawl scene complete with bikers, Burt insisted that he direct it, since he had more experience with this kind of scene than Henry. Paul and Henry decided things would go a lot smoother if they allowed it, so they did. Burt insisted that we fly in Victoria Bolt, a stuntwoman from Los Angeles, to do the scene where he throws the girl biker over the bar. The producers did not want to do this because of the added expense, so Burt flew her in and she roomed with me.

Unfortunately, when Burt threw her over the bar, she landed headfirst into a huge beam, knocking a hole in her head and sending her to the emergency room. Paul Maslansky and I were with her, and Paul was furious. He was not happy with the whole scene and he was especially upset with the injury. He was genuinely concerned with the girl's well-being and didn't want to leave the hospital. I told him to go on home, because he had an early call and that I'd stay with her until she was allowed to leave. Then she could stay with me until she was well enough to travel back to California.

I called Burt to tell him she was going to be all right and that I was taking her back to my hotel. After she went to bed, I had to awaken her every fifteen minutes during the night because of her concussion to make sure she was okay and to occasionally change her bandages. . . .

After the film wrapped, Burt appeared on the *Tonight Show* and gave his opinion of Henry Winkler as a director. He commented that being directed by Winkler was like being directed by Thumper.

Cop And A Half didn't break any box office records

but did respectably in video. However, even with all the problems we had during the filming, I wouldn't have traded the experience for anything.

Burt's Hair

"Do you really work for Burt Reynolds? Does he really wear a wig?" I couldn't believe the pretty contestant in the Miss Florida Teen U.S.A Pageant I was judging in 1988 was asking me this question during a one-on-one session.

"Are your breasts real?" I asked, glancing down at her low-cut dress and back up to the startled look on her face. "I want you to know that kind of question is inappropriate, and I trust you are embarrassed enough by my response to not make that kind of mistake again."

I know everything about Burt Reynolds except what he looks like nude or without his hair. I still can't believe how many people ask me about his hair. Burt usually chose to change his hairpiece either by himself or have his hairdresser do it. When he was getting the hair from Ed Katz and allowing Ed to style it, it always was much more natural. Unfortunately, he started allowing his makeup artist to cut the hairpiece as well as style it, and it has never looked natural since.

Burt's hair has always been a source of major discomfort and embarrassment to him. I personally never mentioned it except to say on occasion, "You've got it too far down on your forehead," or "It needs trimming in the back or on the sides."

When we did the road show, I helped him with his makeup and hair because his makeup guy did not travel with us. Actually, Burt and I did a pretty good job, but then it was for the stage and not the camera, which misses nothing. When the new hairpiece arrived by Federal Express to the hotel where we were freshening up, Burt went into the bathroom and placed it on his head, then came out for approval. I would occasionally trim it a little and then glue the sides down with spirit gum.

One night on the road, I think it was in Memphis, Tennessee, Loni joined us. When she came into the dressing room, I was finishing Burt's makeup and began combing his hair. I caught a glimpse of her in the mirror as she watched me. It must have appeared to her a very tender scene with the gentle stroking of the comb and my patting his hair into place. I suddenly felt for the first time *ever* that I was violating the intimacy a woman has for her man. I turned and handed her the comb and said, "I don't know why I'm doing this now that you're here. I'm sure you're better at it than I." I turned then to select his wardrobe from the closet for that night's performance. She was very quiet and rather solemn, which was unlike her. Any other time, she would have been standing at the mirror beside him freshening her own makeup and chatting away.

He said to her, "That's fine now, I have to get dressed."

I left the two of them in his dressing room, but I couldn't get her look of concern out of my mind as I walked over to my position backstage.

After the road show ended and we were back in California doing *Evening Shade*, I mentioned his hair to her and let her know that I had never seen him without it.

She said to me with a smile, "I know. I'm the only woman Burt has been with who has seen him without his hair."

I knew better, because Pam Seals, Burt's girlfriend, had traveled with us for a while and she told me that he had let her see him without it and she had helped him place it.

Burt's hairpieces cost $1500 each, and he had to have a new one every week. The producers on *Evening Shade* constantly complained about the expense. According to Ed Katz, the designer of the hairpiece, each "unit" should have lasted a month, but Burt had it in his contract that he got a new one every week. Actually he needed it, because he was constantly scratching at it with his fingernails or a pen or pencil and tearing it up.

The same concern came from the "budget patrol" on the movie *Cop and a Half.* "What the hell is this $1500 per unit each week?" the production manager on the film asked me.

" 'Unit' is the term used for Burt's hairpiece and

he needs a new one every week because they don't
last any longer," I explained.

"Jesus Christ!" he said. "The wig only lasts a
week? What does he do with the old ones, make
fur coats?"

I explained that it was a "unit of hair" not a
wig and that it was part of his contract, so he was
entitled to them.

Paul Maslansky, the producer on the film, was
in the room with us and said with a laugh, "I guess
the difference is that a unit costs $1500 and a wig
costs ten bucks."

He's about right. I don't know where Burt is
getting them now, but they surely do not look real.

One evening last year I was relaxing in my bedroom and watching television and the phone rang.

"Is he out of his mind!" I recognized the voice
of a celebrity. "What the hell is he doing? He's
dressed like a fag, his face is all swollen, and what
the hell is that on his head? I can't believe he's
doing this. Why is he airing his laundry in public?
First the *Enquirer* and now on national television?!"

Burt was appearing on "Good Morning America
at Night" in an interview with Chantal shortly after exposing his affair with his girlfriend, Pam
Seals, in the *National Enquirer.* During the interview
he announced that he'd like Loni to take a sodium
pentothal test to find out how many illicit affairs
she had been having. He was wearing a horrible
purple suit, purple shirt, and purple tie. On his
head was "the Harpo Marx wig" as everyone re-

ferred to it. Even I couldn't defend that one because it was so bad.

Hopefully one day soon, he'll decide a hairpiece is just too much trouble to deal with and will be happy with his own natural good looks. It certainly works for Sean Connery and a lot of other guys.

The Hollywood Shuffle

Dick Clayton is by far one of the finest people in the entertainment business. He is well respected in the industry and is truly a gentleman. He was Burt's agent for twenty years and is definitely responsible for getting Burt's career off the ground. Even though Dick left Burt several years ago, our friendship has remained. I speak with him on the phone very often, and we have lunch together as much as possible. We reminisce about the "good ole days" with Burt and how we both still worry about him.

Dick has said so many times, "Elaine, Burt is so talented and right now he should be enjoying this part of his life. It's really sad that things have not gone better for him." He's right. Burt has worked hard for so many years and really is angry about his life at this point. He basically is a good soul, but is his own worst enemy.

I spoke with Larry Bishop (Joey Bishop's son) recently, who is a very talented writer and is currently directing one of his original screenplays *Trig-*

ger Happy, starring Richard Dreyfuss. Larry first brought *Trigger Happy* to our office at Burt Reynolds Productions for Burt to play the lead.

Burt was very excited about doing the film, so Larry came to the set of *Cop and a Half* with Harry Uflan and the head of the movie division of HBO. Burt and I met the three of them at a local restaurant in Tampa. I could tell right away that Burt did not like the guy from HBO, and at a certain point, he jumped up from the table and yelled at him. Words were exchanged in anger and Burt left the room. I walked out with him and said, "You go on to the car, I want to explain something to him."

"Don't go in there and apologize for me. I'm right this time and you know it."

"Yep, you surely are, and I need to explain that to him." I went back into the meeting.

The guy from HBO looked at me and said, "I've never had an actor talk to me that way!"

"Well, Mr. Reynolds was sitting in front of you being as humble as possible, selling himself, which is difficult under the best of circumstances, and you popped up in the middle of his sentence and made a comment about having to 'schlepp all the way to Florida.' It was a bit disrespectful, to say the least," I explained.

"Well, I didn't mean just because of meeting with him. Schlepp is a word I use all the time, everybody does," he said.

"Well, he thought you meant it literally and so did I, because that's the reason you're here. I'm really sorry this happened, because he would be wonderful in this role. Maybe we can work it out when he settles down."

"Okay, I'm sorry, too. We'll be in touch."

Burt did want to pursue the film, but he didn't want that particular guy to be involved, so it never happened.

During that same summer of 1992, Burt, Scott, and I had gone to Dollywood, Dolly Parton's famous theme park and resort, to do Burt's one-man show.

"Honey, have you met Bobby Goldsboro yet?" Burt asked me and introduced us. "Bobby and Diane live in Ocala not too far from Tampa (we were still filming *Cop and a Half*), so he's coming down to see us on the set."

"Great, I'll be looking forward to it," I said to them.

"I come over to Tampa quite often to edit my animated videos. So, if you like, you can come to the studio and see what we're doing. I just told Burt about a new children's Halloween show I'm producing, and he's interested in getting involved and wants you to take a look at it," Bobby said.

"Super," I said. "I have five grandsons, so you can see that I love the idea already."

When we got back to Tampa, Bobby called and I met him at the studio, and we discussed plans for Burt's involvement. I told him that Burt wanted to create a new division of Burt Reynolds Productions and name it "Goldsboro/Reynolds Productions." He was really excited about the project and began to tell me about his already successful animated films.

After my meeting with Bobby I filled Burt in on all the ideas Bobby and I had discussed. He was very enthusiastic and wanted me to spearhead the project. Bobby's newest endeavor was in the beginning stages and Burt felt we would be in a good position to get it off the ground. It was a pilot for a series of animated shows, so I made the necessary contacts at CBS and arranged for Bobby and me to pitch the project when we got back to California.

Burt asked me to find a small work space as soon as I got back to California so we would have an office outside of our offices at *Evening Shade*. I began to search in the area of MTM/CBS Studios where we were filming *Evening Shade*, to make it more convenient for Burt and me both to work between the locales. I located the space and even had a sign for the new company sandblasted as Burt had instructed, right down to the maroon and gold colors of Florida State University that he always wanted on everything.

I worked for a week, getting ready for *Evening Shade* and setting up the new office. I had received letters and phone calls from Bobby since I had come back, and we were both looking forward to the meeting with CBS.

It never happened.

After the change on *Evening Shade* Burt's friend of over twenty years, Snuff Garrett, who had been musical director on the show and had written and produced its theme song was replaced by Bobby Goldsboro.

The Goldsboro/Reynolds Productions never materialized and *Evening Shade* was canceled that same year.

It Never Ends

"Burt's filing for a divorce in Florida," the voice on the other end of the phone said, "but nobody's supposed to know about it."

"That's a joke," I replied. "I've already heard it from two people on *Evening Shade*. One of Burt's people, who is handling part of it, told a couple of people confidentially, who told a couple of people on the q.t., who told . . . God, probably the only person who doesn't know it yet is Loni."

"Oh, she suspects, but I don't know if she knows it's going to happen this soon," the voice on the other end of the wire said.

"Well, knowing Burt, he won't face her. He'll have someone else do it for him," I continued. "I'm just glad I'm not working for him right now, I'd probably have to be the one to break it to her."

I was very disappointed in him for announcing the breakup of his marriage in the *National Enquirer.* I felt, as many of his close friends did, that he should have allowed Loni to announce it. It would not have been a bad idea to have called the press and simply stated that the two of them were ending their marriage and respectfully request the press and public to allow them as much privacy as possible. Expressing that it was very painful to both of them and, more importantly, their four-year-old son, Quinton—everyone would have understood.

Unfortunately, Burt makes it very difficult for those surrounding him to disagree with him. They are all afraid of losing their "position" with him and have "yes sir'd" him to death . . . almost literally. He and I had many confrontations over the years, over his abuse of prescribed drugs, losing his temper and lashing out at top industry people, and even choices of plays at his theatre. I sincerely wish someone had said to him, "Boss, maybe you shouldn't do it this way, maybe the better way would be to call a press conference."

He is not unreasonable when approached this way. He has written brutal letters to network executives when he was angry, but I always typed a rough draft as dictated, read it aloud to him, and suggested a way to express it a little more diplomatically. He usually would give in and say, "You're right. It does get the point across and I just want to explain my side, but I'd like to punch the sonovabitch anyway."

* * *

I received a call from Lois Armstrong, a reporter for *People* magazine during Loni and Burt's tabloid divorce exposé. "Burt Reynolds gave me your number and asked me to call and you would tell me the truth about the breakup," she said.

"Just what do you want to know?" I asked. She wanted me to say who I thought was at fault, and didn't I feel the public had been deceived by their appearance of being the perfect happy couple. "Well, I will not say anything bad about either of them. I just know that Burt loves his little boy dearly, and he's the most important person in Burt's life. As for the public being deceived, it is a simple case of a marriage that didn't work. Didn't you ever have a fight with your husband or boyfriend either before you left home or on the way to a party, and by the time you got there you either could kill each other or were not speaking to each other? Yet when you walked into the room, you both smiled and were just wonderful in front of everyone, not wanting to spoil the gaiety or embarrass yourselves. You either made up during the party or smiled as you said your goodbyes and got into the car and never said a word to each other on the way home? It's the same way with them. Here are two people who choose not to be married to each other anymore, so what's the big deal? They are high-profile celebrities, so it's harder to mask."

"I guess I never thought about it that way, but you're right," said Lois.

* * *

"I can't believe it!" It was Pam Seals, calling from her home in Lutz, Florida, in 1993. "They really set me up. You know I told you over a week ago when we were having lunch that I was going to Tampa to visit my mother, because I hadn't seen her since Christmas. Well, when I got to the airport in Los Angeles on Friday, the *National Enquirer* reporters were all over me. They were asking about my breakup with Burt and to respond as to how I felt about his sending me back to Tampa. I told them that I was only going home to visit my mother and I'd be back in a week or so. A reporter said, 'We were told by Burt Reynolds's representative, Scott Jackson, that the relationship had ended and Burt was sending you back to Florida.' Well, I only have two bags with me, so I'd better go back to the house and get the other twenty!" she replied to the reporter.

She was very upset, but I had already heard the rumor that they'd broken up and she was sent home. I knew this scene, and I also knew what had transpired on the set of *Evening Shade* the day of her departure, so I knew she was the "excuse" of the moment.

I had gone over to meet Jim and Carol Hampton because we were going out after the filming to a local jazz club. When I arrived on the set, one of the crew members came up to me and said, "Have you heard what has been happening with Burt this week?"

"Well," I replied, "I ran into one of the camera crew this week and they said Burt and the director, John Ratzenberger (formerly the mailman on *Cheers*), were not getting along and that Burt was making some pretty snide remarks to him all week and at one point did a mock swing and caught his glasses and knocked them off his face.

"He also said that everyone was afraid that if Burt didn't settle down, they'd all be out of a job because CBS was only going to tolerate so much of this kind of behavior.

"Today, all hell broke loose and he went wild . . . he said it was because Pam had left him, but I heard that he sent her back to Florida because she had become too bossy."

"Bull," I said, "Pam told me a week ago when we had lunch that she was going home to see her mom because she hadn't seen her since Christmas. It's just an excuse for his behavior. He's so angry with himself that he takes it out on everyone else and blames the person closest to him."

I related this to Pam and told her that I knew the first thing Scott and Lamar did was to cover Burt's actions, so she got to be the scapegoat. "Scott probably called the *Enquirer* and tipped them off about you going to Florida so it would provide the smoke screen they needed."

"He did call and ask my flight information before I left, and the reporter did say Scott gave them the information. It just hurts to think he'd do that to me."

"Scott was just doing what he thought he was

supposed to do. Your feelings do not matter to any of them when the heat is on. Scott and Lamar will do whatever is necessary to protect their position with Burt, regardless of who gets hurt."

"I'll Always Be There for You!"

It was June in 1992 during the filming of *Cop and a Half* in Tampa, Florida, when Burt told me that he was going to have to shut down the Burt Reynolds Productions office in L.A. for financial reasons and let everyone go. "You'll be back on *Evening Shade's* payroll sometime in August and when we can get on our feet again, we can start up the office and maybe bring everyone back," he explained to me.

"That's okay, Boss," I said understandingly. "We've weathered these storms before and survived."

I was fine until Burt's attorney, Tom Rowan, called from Los Angeles. "We're going to keep Lamar on payroll until *Evening Shade* starts back up. Burt said that since you're married, you've got somebody to take care of you so you can do without a paycheck for a couple of months until the show starts."

"What?" I yelled. "How dare he say that. He knows very well that I have always paid my own living expenses. No man has ever taken care of me. Even when I was divorced and lived in one of Burt's condos, I paid the rent and all the utilities!" I was so angry and hurt that Burt would even think of saying such a thing. It wasn't so much doing without the money. I knew I had enough to tide me over until August. It was his inference that "you have to be a man or have a man to take care of you in order to survive." In retrospect, I probably overreacted, but I guess I felt Burt, of all people, should understand my situation.

I was in Burt's dressing room the next day and he told me that Tom had told him everything I said, and he got very angry with me.

"I've always been there for you, Elaine, and I'll always be there for you!" Burt said.

When I got back to L. A. and went into my office at the studio, I began trying to catch up and prepare for the first episode of the next season on *Evening Shade*. I had been working with Lamar the whole week and he never gave any indication of what was in store for me. He just smiled and acted like everything was fine, and even though I had already heard there was a major budget cut, I wasn't prepared for the news.

Burt had come into the office several days that week and appeared to be very upset. He told me that he found out that Loni had been seeing other men while he was in Florida and that was why he was upset. On Thursday Burt just hugged me for no apparent reason and never let on that something was up. Friday morning I was going through some papers when Doug Jackson and Tommy Thompson (two producers on the show) came into the reception area. This was the first time I had seen them since I had returned to L. A. I walked out of my office and gave them each a hug, as I really liked these guys, and we all walked into Lamar's office. I was joking as I always did, but both appeared very somber.

"Elaine," Doug began, "you know CBS has been pressuring us to cut the budget on this show and the bottom line is, we've had to cut the associate producer's position." The words shot through me like a burning bullet. "Burt is very upset about this which is why he isn't here today, but it's a done deal, so there is no reason to contact him to try to get him to reverse the decision."

I was numb, but I maintained control (I had become quite good at this over the years) and said, "Doug, I know how hard it was for you to tell me this. I'm really shocked, but I understand. I will accept this as a budget cut decision, but I must say I'm sorry to leave the show. I know I contributed a lot these past two seasons and I was really looking forward to this year, but I understand. I already know about not contacting Burt, because he can never deal with this kind of situation."

I stood up to leave and said to each of them as they hugged me, "Thank you both for all the support you gave me when I first came here and I'll really miss you guys." I went back into my office and closed the door.

No Burt Reynolds Productions, no *Evening Shade,*

no regular paycheck . . . no more marriage (it had been going down the tube for the past two years and earlier in the week we had decided to get a divorce), and no more security. The anger, the pain, the depression, and fear all came at once as I started to clean out my desk.

Burt couldn't face me, so he stayed home the day I got the word. A couple of days later, John Spring said he had overheard Loni yelling at Burt, "Is Elaine finally gone?!"

"Yes," Burt said, "she's gone, are you satisfied?"

In August 1993, Ken, the man I was dating, was invited by Burt to join him for the Golden Boot Awards ceremony. These awards honor people who have played a significant role in Western films and this particular year, Pat Buttram, Clint Eastwood, Roy Rogers and Dale Evans, Jane Fonda and Ted Turner, Melissa Gilbert and Bruce Boxleitner were among the celebrities attending. The money raised is donated to the Television and Motion Pictures Actors Home.

When I talked with Burt the week before, he explained, "Pam (Seals) will be out here and since we haven't really started appearing in public together yet, the press would drive us crazy. I've invited Doug McClure and some of the guys for a 'boys' night out' and you and Pam can go out to dinner or something and we'll all get together afterwards at my house."

When Ken came over the day before the awards,

I told him that an itinerary had been faxed to my house while he was en route and the plans had changed. Burt's father and sister had come in from Florida and were going to the awards ceremony. When he saw the itinerary showing the table of eleven, including Charles Durning and his wife, as well as Bobby Goldsboro and his wife, Ken said, "Well I'm taking you."

"I can't go, because his sister is going to be there," I explained. "But, hey, It's okay. I've been doing this for fifteen years and it doesn't hurt anymore."

"No way, I'm buying you a ticket and we'll sit at another table away from them," said Ken. "You don't work for him anymore, so you don't have to hide from his sister. Anyway, I don't care about sitting with Burt Reynolds, I want to sit with you."

With that he picked up the phone and dialed Burt's home number. Scott Jackson, his assistant, took the call. Ken said, "Please tell Burt thank you for the invitation, but since the plans have changed, I'm taking Elaine. She explained about his sister, so our table is well away from his. Just tell him I'll drop by and say hello."

A call came back immediately. "Burt's so upset. If Elaine shows up, his sister will walk out," said Scott.

"And nobody will even notice or care. There will probably be a thousand people there and they won't be watching the 'Nancy and Elaine Show'!" responded Ken.

I could just picture Burt stomping around in his

bedroom, banging his fist on the bathroom counter, throwing himself on the bed—I've been there, seen that—yelling, "How could Elaine do this to me after all I've done for her?"

Some of the painful feelings from the past were starting to come back when the phone rang again. I answered the phone and the voice at the other end, said, "Elaine, this is Pam." She was still in Florida. " 'Mister' is so upset. He can't believe you would hurt him like this. You know how his sister is and she will walk out. So he said, if you go, the friendship is off."

"Hurt *HIM?!* What friendship?!!" I yelled back into the phone. "I've been his friend and mother for twenty years and he hasn't been my friend for twenty minutes."

Ken took the receiver from me and began talking with Pam. When he hung up, he said, "Did you know that Burt hasn't even talked to her, that he had Scott call her to tell her to call you, and by the way, why does she call him 'Mister'? Boy, I just don't get it! I know I probably won't be able to get through on the phone to tell him personally after tonight, so I'm going to send him a letter telling him exactly what I think of this whole deal."

"Don't waste your time," I said. "Even if the letter is given to him, which it probably won't be, he won't read it because he knows he's wrong."

I got dressed for the Golden Boot Awards, and Ken and I had a wonderful time. Ken had chosen a table quite a distance from Burt's party and we never even saw them.

I went back to the set a couple of times to watch the filming and once I went into Burt's dressing room. His guys around him had a stunned look on their faces as I walked past them and motioned for them to leave. Burt hugged me very tightly and said, "I just miss you so much. I don't know how I'm going to get along without you. Are you okay?"

"Yep," I lied, "I'm fine, Burt." Funny, that was the first time I called him Burt in years. "I just stopped in to check on you, so I have to go now." I left his dressing room and went home. I couldn't bear to sit through the show that night and I didn't ever go back again.

We still spoke on the phone occasionally and Burt would tell me that it was better if no one in the office knew we were talking, because they were all so "paranoid" that I might be coming back. They needn't have been concerned, as I never had any intention of going back.

After leaving the show, I think I miss postproduction most of all. During 1993 I was invited by Harry on several occasions to attend the filming of *Hearts Afire*. Some of the former camera crew on *Evening Shade* had moved over to this show and they always came up and gave me a hug and told me how much they missed me and how "out of control" Burt had become.

Part of me said, *Thank God I don't have to take care*

of him anymore, and the other part wanted to "save" him by getting him into a rehab center like the Betty Ford Clinic, because I knew he couldn't save himself. When Pam would call and say, "Burt wants to talk to you, but he doesn't want to talk about what happened when you left," I knew that already. He can never face anyone under those circumstances and he only said to me, "I know you didn't do anything wrong, but it's already done now." He would talk about his divorce from Loni and how it was killing him financially, but his fear of not seeing as much of Quinton upset him the most.

One night I came home about 11:30 and a message was on my answering machine from Pam. "Burt needs to talk with you as soon as possible, so please call him as soon as you get in. He's going to bed around 10:30, so call if you get home before that time." I called the next morning and she said, "Where were you, he really needed to talk to you last night."

"Frankly, I had a date and it was a free meal, so I went out, okay? Besides I don't work for him anymore and I don't have to check in every ten minutes." I can't believe I actually felt guilty when I hung up. It took over a year to finally let go.

My daughter Lori recently sent me a card that had a beautiful picture of the moon with ashes below that simply said, "My barn having burned to the ground, I can now see the moon." Inside was written, "Burt was your barn, now reach for the moon."

I have to say that I really loved my "barn" and I do miss him. I was very lucky to have had so many exciting roads to travel over my seventeen years with Burt, and all the interesting—though sometimes painful—experiences I shared with him are ever present in my mind.

When I am asked if I'd ever go back and work for Burt again if he wanted me, my answer is, "Not as an employee . . . but if he *really* needed me in a crisis, I'd be there in a flash."

My life has become my own now. I currently have a movie of the week in at CBS and will be filming a feature in Spain with Budd Boetticher. Now that I have expressed my innermost feelings in this book, I feel I can finally say goodbye to the past and leave it behind. I am happier than I have been in years and I am truly blessed with great friends, good health, a loving family, and a free spirit!